this book
belongs to:

- - - - - - - - - -

IN LOVING
MEMORY OF
MY ABUELO

THANK YOU TO:

David, for your love and support and for happily
eating all the 'recipe testing'.

My sister, Carmen, for your valued feedback on
virtually every page of this book.

My dad, Graham, for happily sharing all the wonderful family
photos you shot many moons ago.

My Mexican family members, for sharing your precious
photos and memories of Abuelo and of the family.

My Abuela, for once again agreeing to share your
precious recipes with the rest of the world.

Hardie Grant, for your continued support of my work.

Last, but not least, to my mum, Elsa, for putting together the recipes and
sharing many memories of Abuelo that make this book what it is.

MY ABUELO'S MEXICAN FEAST

by

Daniella Germain

with

Elsa Germain

hardie grant books

MELBOURNE · LONDON

SBS

CONTENTS

Regalos del mar

COMIDA CALLEJERA

TORTAS

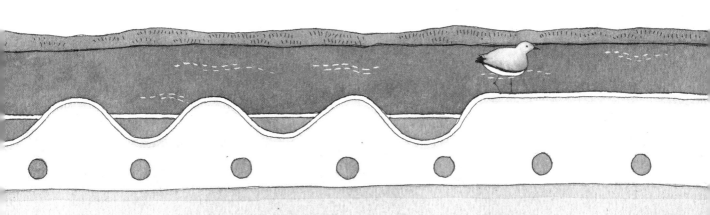

MALECÓN DE ALVARADO

Abuelo with his
young family

Abuela & Abuelo

Abuelo & Mum

PROP.
E.HERMIDA G   " PEDRO CARLO "   JOCKEY
ENT.   JUL.11.1986   H.LEMUS
S.GUTIERREZ   DIST.1milla
                                                                 t.1;45;1

Abuelo owned many
winning racehorses

the accomplished
Surgeon

ABOUT THIS BOOK

My Abuelo's Mexican Feast is a collection of recipes that pays homage to my Abuelo (grandfather). My Abuelo, Elias Hermida González, was an extraordinarily loving, warm, intelligent and talented man who had a wonderfully full life filled with family, a love of animals and his work as a surgeon saving lives.

Although the times my sister, Carmen, and I shared with Abuelo were all too short, with an ocean between us, my memories of him are vivid and full of love. Abuelo affectionately called Carmen 'Grillis' (little crickets) and me 'Koalita' (little koala). He even named some of his racehorses after us! Although his English was not perfect (and our Spanish even worse), we would have fun teaching each other words and he was always interested to know more about our lives even though we were living worlds apart. ·

Most of the recipes in this book are those of my Abuela (grandmother), and some have been in our family for many generations. The recipes are structured around the journey of my Abuelo's life, and the food he loved – from his childhood growing up in the fishing town of Alvarado, to Mexico City, where he gained an education and established his family life and career, enjoying the fruits of his labour.

I hope you enjoy each and every one of these recipes, as well as the stories and photos from my Abuelo's and my family's lives.

Abuela & Abuelo

MEXICO
MAP

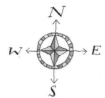

N

W ← E

S

TO THE
USA

GULF
OF
MEXICO

JALISCO

MEXICO
CITY

VERACRUZ
ALVARADO

OAXACA

P A C I F I C   O C E A N

TO SOUTH
↓ AMERICA

A LITTLE HISTORY

Elias Hermida González was born on 25 August 1920 into a hard-working, proud and resilient – but poor – family who were originally from Spain. He was the fifth child and third son (the second son died at an early age) of Roberto Hermida Salas and Luisa María González Bravo. Roberto was the son of Spanish-born Don Miguel Hermida and Feliciana Salas, who arrived in Veracruz in the mid 1800s. Don Miguel had made his living from commercial fishing on the northern coast of Spain and Feliciana was famous for her delicious pastries and cakes, which were always highly in demand at their family bakery business back in Spain. Abuelo used to say that it was Feliciana who introduced the now famous marquezote cake to Alvarado (see page 115).

Abuelo's father, Roberto, was a gifted silversmith. He was commissioned to forge the elegant metalwork, including the many sculptures of angels and the streetlamp poles, that still exist to this day in the *zócalo* (town square) of Alvarado. Roberto was also a wonderful cook and, together with his wife, Luisa, set up a seafood restaurant to supply the growing demands of hungry sailors and the evolving fishing town. In time his restaurant became famous and well patronised by both the community as well as visitors to the town.

My Abuelo tragically lost his mother when he was just seven. He worked selling sweets and pastries as a young boy to help support his family. Sometimes Abuelo would deliver his goods from house to house, targeting the more opulent and well-to-do homes, like the Ochoa family home – although he didn't know he would marry the eldest daughter of Don Octavio César Ochoa almost fifteen years later. The first time they met, my Abuela – a cheeky three-year-old – spoiled most of my Abuelo's tray of meringues by squashing every one of them.

Abuelo also spent much of his childhood helping his father in his modest fishing business in the port of Alvarado in the Gulf of Mexico. Abuelo beat the odds of his social disadvantage by learning to read and write at the age of fifteen, and eventually enrolled at the Universidad Nacional Autónoma de México in Mexico City to study medicine.

Abuelo said that becoming a doctor would help to save other children's mothers – his own mother was unable to be saved because of the lack of doctors in the little town of Alvarado. Not only did he become a celebrated doctor, he also helped and inspired others to achieve their dreams and goals, including his own children and grandchildren. We have many doctors in our family and I'm sure this is largely due to the exceptional role model that my Abuelo was.

Several years later, nearing the end of his medical studies, Abuelo returned to Alvarado impeccably dressed and successful. He had only one purpose for his return: to court my Abuela, who was now an eighteen-year-old beauty. They were smitten with each other and were married soon after. They eventually returned to Mexico City where they began their life together.

Abuelo and Abuela went on to have a bustling household with seven children: Elias, Carmen, Elsa (my mum), Beatriz, Laura, Juan Carlos and Alejandra (Jana). Abuelo relished his family life, spending much time at La Granja (a farm outside Alvarado) and Los Arrayanes (a ranch in Querétaro, outside Mexico City) with his family and beloved horses. Many of my memories of Abuelo are of the times shared at these places, and the smell of horses always takes me back to those happy times.

Sadly we lost Abuelo in 2001, so he will not get to see this book, which is a tribute to his memory, remarkable life journey and, of course, passion for food.

Regalos del mar

GIFTS OF THE SEA

My Abuelo was born and raised in the seaside town of Alvarado in the state of Veracruz on the southeast coast of Mexico. His parents, Roberto and Luisa, owned and ran a small but successful seafood restaurant, which was hugely popular among locals and visitors alike.

When he was young, Abuelo helped out in the restaurant. Each day he would jump on a *piragua*, a traditional handmade fishing boat, and row to his favourite spots. He loved fishing and would call seafood *regalos del mar* ('gifts of the sea'). He would also check the handmade nets for the catch of the day, which often consisted of shiny blue crabs as large as melons, ghost-like transparent prawns (shrimp), and sometimes lobsters. Abuelo would supply his parents' tiny restaurant with the freshest seafood, which would also become dinner for his brother and sisters.

The following recipes are very old family recipes, many of which were cooked in Abuelo's parents' restaurant.

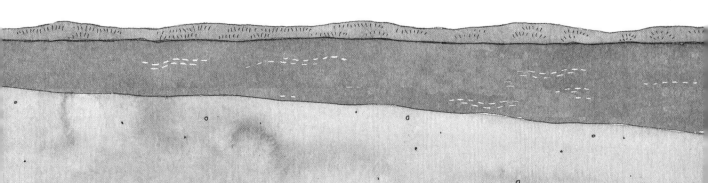

Cóctel de mariscos

·seafood cocktail·

500 g (1 lb 2 oz) small cooked prawns
   (shrimp)
250 g (9 oz) fresh oysters
250 g (9 oz) cooked crabmeat
juice of 2 limes
1 tomato, chopped
125 ml (4 fl oz/½ cup) olive oil
125 ml (4 fl oz/½ cup) tomato juice
125 ml (4 fl oz/½ cup) tomato sauce
   (ketchup)
½ bunch bulb spring onions (scallions),
   finely chopped
½ bunch of coriander (cilantro)
   leaves, roughly chopped, plus
   extra for garnish
60 ml (2 fl oz/¼ cup) chipotle sauce
2 avocados, cut into cubes
lime cheeks to serve
crackers to serve

Mix all the seafood in a large bowl.

Add the remaining ingredients, except
the avocado, extra coriander, lime and
crackers, and stir gently until combined.
Season to taste.

Spoon the seafood mix into 6 tall cocktail
glasses, topping each glass with some
avocado and the extra coriander leaves.

Serve with the lime cheeks and crackers.

Serves 6

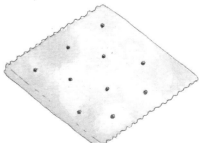

Ceviche

· marinated fish ·

500 g (1 lb 2 oz) semi-firm white fish,
    such as sea bass or red snapper
juice of 3 lemons
2 teaspoons salt
2 large ripe tomatoes, chopped
1 small onion,. finely chopped
15 g (½ oz/¼ cup) finely chopped
    coriander (cilantro) leaves
2 tablespoons finely chopped red chilli
2 tablespoons olive oil
8 black olives, sliced (optional)
1 small avocado, cubed
corn (tortilla) chips or crackers
    to serve

Dice the fish into 1 cm (½ in) cubes.

Toss the fish, lemon juice and salt in a non-metallic mixing bowl. Cover and marinate for 5 hours or overnight in the refrigerator.

When ready to serve, combine the remaining ingredients, except the olives, avocado and corn chips, in a separate bowl.

Drain the fish and discard the lemon juice.

Combine the fish with the tomato mixture and place on a serving platter. Top with the olives, if using, and avocado and serve with the corn chips or crackers.

Serves 6

serving suggestion

Sopa de almejas

· clam soup ·

When Abuelo returned from his fishing expeditions he would often present his sisters (who took over the role of their mother after her death) with a bowl of pipis or small clams (vongole) that were the main ingredient of this fragrant, herby soup.

1.5 kg (3 lb 5 oz) fresh small clams (vongole)
  in their shells
1 dried poblano chilli
200 g (7 oz) butter
2 garlic cloves, finely chopped
1 large white onion, finely chopped
2 large ripe tomatoes, peeled and chopped
¼ teaspoon dried oregano
½ teaspoon dried marjoram
1.5 litres (51 fl oz/6 cups) fish or chicken stock
olive oil to drizzle
crusty baguette to serve

Scrub the clams well under running water and set aside.

Dry-roast the chilli in a frying pan over a medium–high heat until its natural oil is released and it has puffed up. Remove the chilli from the pan and, when cool enough to handle, remove the membrane and seeds before chopping finely.

In a medium saucepan, melt the butter over a medium heat. Add the garlic, onion and chilli and fry gently for a few minutes until softened. Add the tomato, dried herbs and stock. Bring to the boil then reduce the heat to low and simmer for 20 minutes. Add the clams and simmer for a further 5 minutes or until the clams have opened. Discard any unopened clams.

Season then serve hot with a splash of olive oil and the crusty bread.

Serves 4

Empanadas de jaiba

· crab empanadas ·

60 ml (2 fl oz/¼ cup) extra-virgin olive oil
½ white onion, finely chopped
4 garlic cloves, finely chopped
1 teaspoon dried oregano
2 small red chillies, finely chopped
2 large ripe tomatoes, peeled and
    chopped
8 green olives, pitted and sliced

1 bay leaf
juice of 1 lime
500 g (1 lb 2 oz) fresh uncooked
    crabmeat
2 sheets of frozen puff pastry, thawed
1 beaten egg for glazing

Preheat the oven to 180°C (350°F).

Heat the olive oil in a heavy frying pan over a medium heat and sauté the onion and garlic until translucent. Add the remaining ingredients, except the crab, pastry and egg. Cook for 5 minutes until the tomatoes start to soften. Reduce the heat to low and simmer for 5 minutes.

Add the crabmeat, cover and cook for 5–7 minutes. When the crab is cooked turn the heat off and allow to cool.

Assemble the empanadas by cutting each pastry sheet into 4 equal portions. Using a small bowl as a guide, cut a circle about 15 cm (6 in) in diameter from each pastry piece. Place 2 tablespoons of the crab mixture on half of each pastry round, leaving a 1 cm (½ in) border from the edge of the pastry. Moisten the pastry edges with a little of the beaten egg and fold over the pastry to create a half-circle shape.

Press the edges closed with a fork to achieve the traditional look of the empanada. Prick the empanadas a few times with a fork to create holes for the steam to escape.

Brush the empanadas with the beaten egg and bake for 15–20 minutes or until golden and the pastry is cooked. Serve hot or cold.

Makes 8 empanadas

Variation: Use fresh prawns (shrimp) instead of crab to make *empanadas de Vigilia* (empanadas eaten during Lent).

Sopa de langostinos con bolitas

· prawn soup with corn dumplings ·

For the soup:

1 litre (34 fl oz/4 cups) fish stock

4 fish heads, backbones and tails

2 carrots, sliced

1 large onion

4 garlic cloves, smashed

1 bay leaf

3 black peppercorns

*500 g (1 lb 2 oz) raw large prawns (shrimp),
    peeled and deveined, tails left on*

For the sauce:

6 green poblano chillies, seeded

*60 g (2 oz/1 cup) finely chopped flat-leaf
    (Italian) parsley*

*50 g (1¾ oz/1 cup) chopped coriander
    (cilantro) leaves and stalks*

1 bunch of basil

½ white onion

4 garlic cloves

*60 ml (2 fl oz/¼ cup) fish stock from soup
    (see above)*

60 ml (2 fl oz/¼ cup) extra-virgin olive oil

For the dumplings:

*500 g (1 lb 2 oz) masa dough
    for tortillas (page 72)*

60 g (2 oz) lard

Place all the soup ingredients, except the prawns, in a large saucepan or stockpot and bring to the boil over a high heat. Reduce the heat to low and simmer for 45 minutes. Strain the stock into a clean saucepan.

To make the sauce, place all the sauce ingredients, except the olive oil, in a blender and process until smooth.

In a small, deep saucepan, heat the olive oil and fry the sauce over a medium heat, stirring constantly, for 5 minutes or until thickened slightly.

Bring the soup to the boil over a high heat and then reduce to low and simmer while the dumplings are being prepared.

To make the dumplings, in a small bowl, beat the masa and lard together using an electric mixer until it becomes light and fluffy. Take tablespoonfuls of the masa mixture and drop them in the boiling soup. The dumplings will be cooked when they float to the surface. Add the prawns and continue cooking for about 5 minutes or until the prawns have turned pink.

Serve the soup in individual bowls, placing a few prawns and masa dumplings in each and topping with 2 teaspoons of the sauce.

Serves 4–6

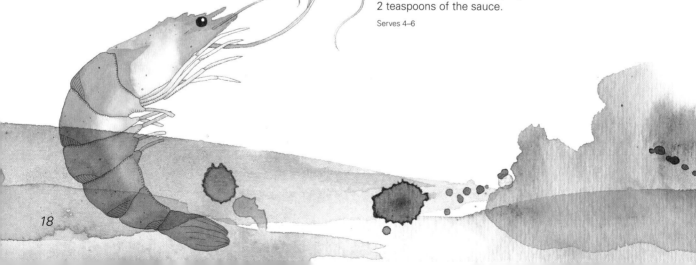

Sopa de tortuga sin tortuga

· mock turtle soup ·

Abuelo grew up eating all kinds of gifts from the sea, including sea turtles. When he was young, catching sea turtles was very difficult and their numbers were not threatened. These days eating sea turtles is uncommon. This classic turtle soup recipe can be made using firm white fish or even crocodile meat as substitutes.

60 ml (2 fl oz/¼ cup) extra-virgin olive oil
1 large white onion, finely chopped
½ garlic bulb, unpeeled
3 large ripe tomatoes, chopped
2 bay leaves
2 cloves
5 pink peppercorns
5 basil leaves
1 teaspoon dried marjoram
1 small green chilli, finely chopped
400 g (14 oz) tin whole peeled tomatoes
1½ teaspoons salt or chicken stock powder

2 tablespoons white vinegar
1 large carrot, finely chopped
1 slice of stale bread, soaked in water and mashed with a fork
3 litres (101 fl oz/12 cups) fish or chicken stock
4 small potatoes, cut into 2 cm (¾ in) cubes
1 kg (2 lb 3 oz) firm white fish fillets, such as flathead or snapper, cut into 4 cm (1½ in) cubes
crusty bread to serve

Heat the olive oil in a large saucepan or stockpot over a medium heat and add the onion and garlic. Sauté until the onion is translucent. Be careful not to burn the garlic. Add the chopped tomatoes and cook for a further 2 minutes.

Add the remaining ingredients, except the stock, potatoes, fish and crusty bread, and cook for 3–5 minutes or until the tomatoes are reduced and thickened. Add the stock. Bring to the boil then reduce the heat to low and simmer for 20 minutes to allow the flavours to develop.

Add the fish pieces and the potatoes and simmer for a further 10 minutes or until the potatoes are cooked. Serve immediately with crusty bread.

Serves 4

delicious with fish, or even crocodile meat!

Minilla de pescado

pulled fish with olives & tomato

Abuelo about to join friends on a fishing trip

125 ml (4 fl oz/½ cup) extra-virgin olive oil
4 garlic cloves, finely chopped
1 white onion, finely chopped
4 ripe tomatoes, peeled and finely chopped
½ teaspoon dried oregano
1 bay leaf
6 fish fillets, such as whiting or perch
90 g (3 oz/½ cup) whole Spanish olives in brine
2 teaspoons capers
¼ bunch of flat-leaf (Italian) parsley, finely chopped
cooked rice or baguette to serve

Heat the olive oil in a large saucepan over a medium heat. Add the garlic and onion and sauté for 2–3 minutes until the onion is soft and translucent. Add the tomato, oregano and bay leaf and cook for a further 5 minutes.

While the sauce is cooking, cut the fish fillets into 5 cm (2 in) cubes and add them to the sauce. Cook for 7–10 minutes.

While the fish cooks, slice the olives and capers. Add them to the fish along with the parsley. Allow the mixture to cook for another 5 minutes. Adjust the seasoning. Using a fork, break the fish pieces down.

Serve with rice, a baguette or as a tostada topping. You can also use the fish as an empanada filling (see page 17).

Serves 4

Chucumites fritos con ajo

· small sea bass with garlic ·

Chucumites or *guabina* are juvenile sea bass, which were once plentiful in the warm waters of the Gulf of Mexico.

4 small whole sea bass or barramundi
8 garlic cloves
1 teaspoon salt
½ teaspoon coriander seeds
½ teaspoon fennel seeds
juice of 1 lime
250 ml (8½ fl oz/1 cup) olive oil for frying
lime wedges to serve

Pat the fish dry and ensure there are no scales left.

Make 3 long incisions along the body of each fish. Using a mortar and pestle, pound the garlic, salt, coriander and fennel seeds and lime juice to form a paste. Rub the fish with this paste and set aside for at least 30 minutes.

In a deep frying pan heat the olive oil over a high heat until smoking. Fry the fish for 3–4 minutes on each side. Drain on paper towels. Serve immediately with the lime wedges.

Serves 4

arroz a la tumbada

· 'tumbled rice' ·

Originating in Alvarado, arroz a la tumbada has been a favourite in our family for generations. It is a wonderful brothy rice dish that can be made with any seafood on hand. Legend has it that this dish was first created by a fisherman who simply 'tossed together' rice with his catch of the day.

So proud are Alvaradeños of this dish that they hold a festival to celebrate it on the last Sunday in May each year. In fact, on one such Sunday in 2012, the Guinness world record for the largest arroz a la tumbada was set in Alvarado, with the townspeople coming together to cook and share 7000 kg (15,430 lb) of this delicacy.

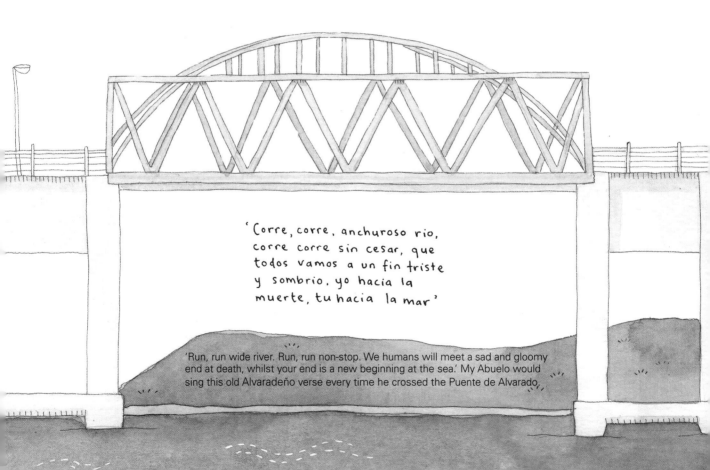

'Corre, corre, anchuroso rio, corre corre sin cesar, que todos vamos a un fin triste y sombrio. yo hacia la muerte, tu hacia la mar'

'Run, run wide river. Run, run non-stop. We humans will meet a sad and gloomy end at death, whilst your end is a new beginning at the sea.' My Abuelo would sing this old Alvaradeño verse every time he crossed the Puente de Alvarado.

75 g (2¾ oz) butter
4 garlic cloves, finely chopped
½ white onion, finely chopped
250 ml (8½ fl oz/1 cup) tomato passata
   (puréed tomatoes)
750 ml (25½ fl oz/3 cups) fish stock
200 g (7 oz) white fish, such as whiting
   or perch
300 g (10½ oz) raw prawns (shrimp),
   peeled and deveined, tails left on
2 large whole crabs
12 clams (vongole), scrubbed and rinsed
4 coriander (cilantro) sprigs
4 flat-leaf (Italian) parsley sprigs

½ teaspoon shrimp paste
juice of 1 lime
lime wedges to serve

For the rice:

100 g (3½ oz) butter
1 tablespoon extra-virgin olive oil
½ white onion, finely chopped
4 garlic cloves, whole
440 g (15½ oz/2 cups) short-grain
   white rice
750 ml (25½ fl oz/3 cups) chicken stock
5 coriander (cilantro) sprigs

To prepare the rice, in a heavy frying pan, heat the butter and olive oil together over a medium heat. Add the onion and garlic, sautéing for 2 minutes. Add the rice to the pan, stirring gently until the rice turns opaque. Be careful not to let the rice go brown. Add the chicken stock and coriander. Bring the stock to the boil, then cover the pan, reduce the heat to low and allow to simmer for 10 minutes – the rice should be slightly undercooked.

Meanwhile, melt the butter in a large pan (a paella dish is ideal) over a medium heat. Add the garlic and onion and sauté for 1–2 minutes. Add the tomato passata and cook for 2–3 minutes. Add the fish stock and the remaining ingredients, except the lime juice and lime wedges. Allow to cook for about 10 minutes – the fish should flake easily with a fork when cooked.

Once cooked, season with salt and pepper and then add the rice to the pan, gently incorporating it into the seafood. Simmer for another 5 minutes or until the rice is tender. Add the lime juice. The result should look similar to a paella, but a little more soupy. Serve immediately, with the lime wedges, in the centre of the table.

Serves 8

PUENTE DE ALVARADO

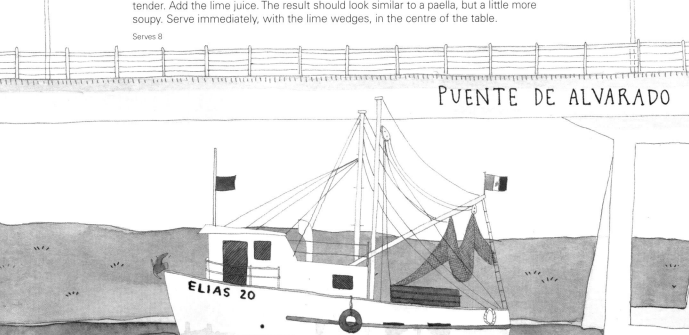

COMIDA
CALLEJERA

STREET FOOD

In 1936 my Abuelo moved to Mexico City to finish his education and follow his calling to become a doctor.

Until his arrival in Mexico City, Abuelo had only known the food of the coastal town of Alvarado, which was mostly seafood. It was a welcome new experience to sample the array of offerings that were to be found on almost every street corner in Mexico City.

Although he worked very hard to put himself through school, Abuelo's salary still barely stretched to feed himself. This is where street food literally became a lifesaver. Cheap but nutritious and freshly made, Abuelo made it his everyday sustenance.

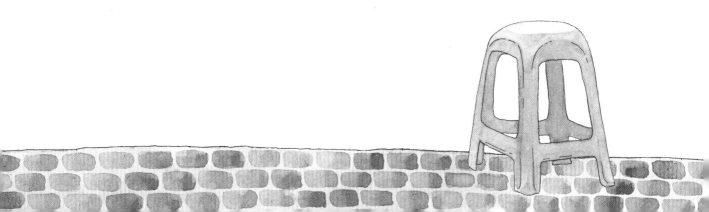

PLÁTANOS FRITOS

·fried bananas·

Plátanos are moreish chips (fries) made from plantain, a type of large banana that is cooked when green to achieve a delicious flavour. These snacks are great with a cold beer on a hot day.

2 teaspoons salt
2 teaspoons chilli powder
4 plantains* or unripe bananas
125 ml (4 fl oz/½ cup) vegetable oil
*   for frying*

* Available from some greengrocers.

Place the salt and chilli powder in a glass jar with a lid. Close the jar and shake until the mixture is combined.

Peel the plaintains and slice them lengthways into 5 mm (¼ in) thick slices.

Heat the vegetable oil in a deep frying pan over a high heat. Fry 4–5 slices at a time for a few minutes or until just golden. Drain on paper towels.

Sprinkle with the salt–chilli mixture and serve immediately.

Serves 4 as a snack

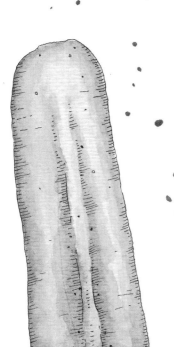

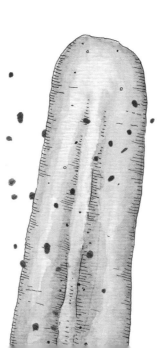

CACAHUATES ENCHILADOS

· lime & chilli peanuts ·

2 teaspoons salt
2 teaspoons chilli powder
2 tablespoons vegetable oil
500 g (1 lb 2 oz) raw skinless peanuts
juice of 1 lime
brown paper cones to serve

Place the salt and chilli powder in a glass jar with a lid. Close the jar and shake until the mixture is combined.

Heat the vegetable oil in a deep frying pan over a high heat. Add the peanuts and stir until well coated with oil. Keep frying for a few minutes until the peanuts start to brown.

Add the lime juice (be careful as this may spit at you) and keep cooking for a couple more minutes until the juice has evaporated and the peanuts are crisp.

Place the peanuts on a large baking tray lined with baking paper.

Sprinkle the nuts with the salt–chilli mixture, stirring with a spoon to ensure every nut is coated.

Allow to cool and then serve in the brown paper cones.

Makes 500 g (1 lb 2 oz)

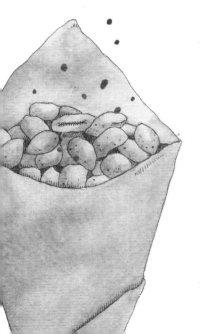

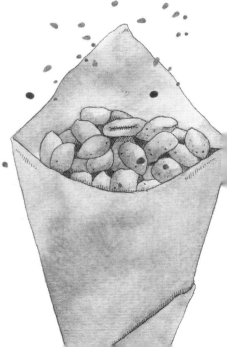

TACOS ASADOS

· pan tacos ·

The simplest but yummiest of snacks.

200 g (7 oz) thick rump steak
1 tablespoon vegetable oil
12 fresh flour tortillas (see page 37, or
 store-bought tortillas can be used)
1 bunch of coriander (cilantro), chopped
¼ white onion, finely chopped
salsa of your choice

Season the steak with salt and pepper.

Heat the vegetable oil in a heavy frying pan over a high heat. Cook the steak for 2–3 minutes on each side or until browned – the meat should still be juicy and pink in the middle when cut with a knife. Chop the steak into strips, set aside and keep warm.

If using fresh tortillas, brush a little water over them and then wrap up a couple at a time in a clean tea towel (dish towel). For store-bought tortillas, just wrap a couple at a time (with no water) in a clean tea towel. Place them in the microwave and cook on high (100%) for 30 seconds.

To serve, place a tortilla on each plate, top with 2–3 strips of beef and scatter over the fresh coriander, onion and salsa.

Makes 12 tacos

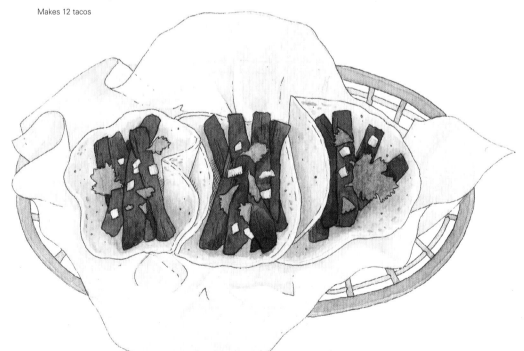

ELOTE CON QUESO
· corn with cheese ·

Elote vendors push large metal drums on wheels filled with steaming hot corn cobs still in their husks, ready to be peeled and smothered in butter, cheese and chilli powder.

4 corn cobs, husks on
4 bamboo skewers
60 g (2 oz) firm butter
75 g (2¾ oz) manchego or mozzarella, grated
chilli powder or chile piquin*

* Available from specialty delicatessens.

With the husks still on, insert skewers into the centre of each corn cob. Cook the corn in plenty of boiling water in a large saucepan for about 15 minutes, allowing the ends of the skewers to stick out of the water.

Place the butter on a plate ready for the hot corn.

Wearing oven gloves, remove the corn cobs from the pan and peel the husks away. Keep the skewers in.

Roll the hot corn cobs in the butter and place them on a serving plate. Sprinkle with the cheese and chilli powder. Eat the corn straight from the skewer.

Serves 4 as a snack

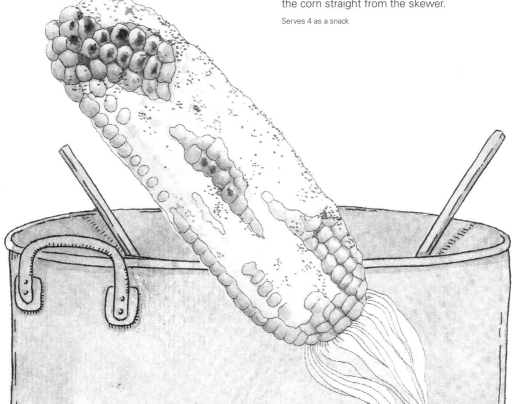

MENUDO

· spicy tripe soup ·

A popular street food in Mexico, menudo is also popular for breakfast, especially after Sunday mass. There is also a widely held belief that menudo is an effective cure for hangovers. Abuelo enjoyed eating it, but never for hangovers. As a conscientious doctor, he did not drink much.

1 kg (2 lb 3 oz) tripe, washed and cut
   into bite-sized pieces
750 g (1 lb 11 oz) pigs' trotters (around
   2 trotters), cut in halves lengthways
6 litres (203 fl oz/24 cups) water
2 white onions, finely chopped, plus
   1 extra, finely chopped, to serve
4 garlic cloves, finely chopped
½ teaspoon freshly ground black pepper
1 teaspoon dried oregano

2 avocado tree leaves*
2 dried guajillo chillies
3 fresh long red chillies, seeded
   and deveined
1 white onion, finely chopped
15 g (½ oz/½ cup) chopped coriander
   (cilantro) leaves
lime wedges

* Available from some greengrocers. 2 fresh basil leaves may be substituted.

Place the tripe and pigs' trotters in a large saucepan or stockpot and add half the water. Bring to the boil over a high heat. Once boiling, turn the heat off and let the meat sit for 5 minutes in the hot water. Drain the liquid and keep the meat in the pan. Add the remaining water to the tripe and pigs' trotters in the pan with the onion, garlic, pepper, oregano and avocado leaves. Bring to the boil over a high heat, then reduce the heat to low and simmer for around 1½ hours.

While the meats are cooking, place the guajillo chillies in a frying pan over a medium–high heat and dry-roast them for a few minutes until the skin begins to char slightly and the natural oils are released. Use an exhaust fan if your kitchen has one as this method may irritate eyes and throats!

Remove the guajillo chillies from the pan and, when cool enough to handle, remove the membranes and seeds. Place the guajillo chillies in a blender with the fresh red chillies and 125 ml (4 fl oz/½ cup) of the tripe liquid (be careful as it will be very hot) and process until the chillies are well blended. Add them to the tripe pan and continue simmering over a low heat for another 1½ hours. Serve the menudo in a deep soup bowl topped with the onion and coriander and a squeeze of lime juice.

Serves 8

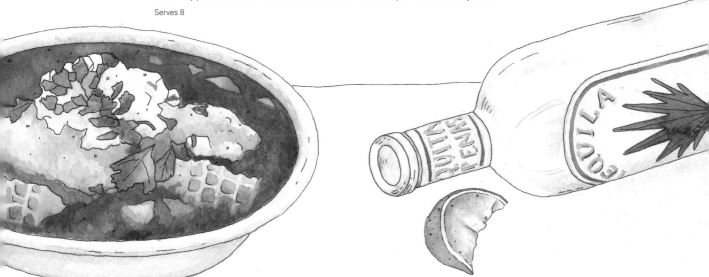

fast food Mexican style

breakfast time in a
Mexican market

¡ salud !

fresh mango...one
of my dad's favourites!

lunch on the run

Mexican market

My sister & Aunty Jana
making sopes!

SOPES

Sopes are the perfect snack and consist of fried tortilla rounds typically topped with beans, queso fresco, lettuce and sour cream.

500 g (1 lb 2 oz) fresh masa dough for tortillas (see page 72)
250 ml (8½ fl oz/1 cup) vegetable oil for frying
460 g (1 lb/2 cups) refried beans
salsa of your choice
300 g (10½ oz/2 cups) grated queso fresco or low-salt feta
125 g (4½ oz/2 cups) finely shredded lettuce
low-fat sour cream (optional)

Shape the masa dough into lime-sized balls. Then, using a tortilla press, form 12 tortillas about 15 cm (6 in) in diameter. If you don't have a tortilla press, roll out the masa between 2 sheets of baking paper with a rolling pin.

Heat the vegetable oil in a small, deep saucepan over a high heat.

Drop each tortilla into the hot oil, one at a time, and fry until the tortilla starts to change colour, about 1 minute. Carefully remove the tortilla from the oil with tongs and drain on paper towels. Once drained, the tortillas can be kept warm by wrapping them in a clean tea towel (dish towel).

Continue cooking the tortillas until all the masa has been used.

When ready to serve, arrange the cooked tortillas on a serving platter. Spread each tortilla with refried beans, top with the salsa of your choice and then the grated cheese, shredded lettuce and sour cream, if using. Season to taste. Serve immediately.

For carnivores, you can add shredded boneless skinless chicken breast, turkey or spicy beef (see opposite).

Makes around 12

Variation: Follow the same method as above but instead of using refried beans, use *pure de papa* (mashed potato) to make *huaraches* ('sandals').

SOPES DE PICADILLO

·spicy beef sopes·

1 tablespoon olive oil
1 garlic clove, finely chopped
1 small red chilli, seeded and thinly
  sliced
¼ white onion, finely chopped
200 g (7 oz) minced (ground) beef
1 bay leaf
½ teaspoon dried oregano
½ teaspoon dried marjoram
3 coriander (cilantro) sprigs
2 tablespoons white vinegar

Heat the olive oil, garlic, chilli and onion in a heavy frying pan over a medium heat and sauté for 2–3 minutes.

Add the beef and fry until golden brown, about 5 minutes. Add the herbs, 190 ml (6½ fl oz/¾ cup) water, the vinegar and season to taste.

Reduce the heat to low and simmer for about 20 minutes or until the meat is tender and the water has evaporated.

Use the beef as a topping on freshly cooked sopes (see opposite).

Makes enough topping for 12 sopes

TAMALES DE ELOTE

· corn tamales ·

For the filling:

625 ml (21 fl oz/2½ cups) water
500 g (1 lb 2 oz) chicken, shin beef or
    pork leg, cut into 5 cm (2 in) cubes
½ white onion, finely chopped
3 garlic cloves
3 pink peppercorns
1 bay leaf
2 whole green chillies, e.g. jalapeños
¼ bunch of coriander (cilantro)
2 tablespoons white vinegar
1 teaspoon salt

For the tamale dough:

10 corn cobs or 750 g (1 lb 11 oz/3¾ cups)
    corn kernels
300 g (10½ oz) lard
1 tablespoon white sugar
1 teaspoon salt
20 g (¾ oz) masa harina for tamales*

For the tamale wrapping:

24–30 dried corn husks**
Salsa verde (page 50) or Salsa roja
    (page 51)
cooking twine or strips of corn husk

* Masa harina is a special flour made from corn, available
at specialty delicatessens. If 'tamale' masa harina is not
available, just use regular masa harina.

** Available from specialist delicatessens.

For the filling, place all the ingredients in a large saucepan or stockpot. Bring to
the boil over a high heat, and then reduce the heat to low and let simmer for about
1½ hours if using beef or pork, or 30 minutes if using chicken.

Once tender, remove the meat from the stock and set aside.

To prepare the tamale dough, if you are using corn cobs, remove the kernels using
a sharp knife.

Place the kernels in a bowl with the lard, sugar and salt. Process with a hand-held
blender until almost completely puréed.

Add the masa harina and mix well using a wooden spoon. The mixture should be the
consistency of toothpaste. Set aside.

To assemble the tamales, take 2 or 3 corn husks and shape them together like the hull
of a canoe. Spread a large tablespoon of the corn mixture into the corn husk 'canoe',
then top with a tablespoon of the cooked meat. Spread a teaspoon of salsa over the
meat, and then add an additional tablespoon of the corn mixture on top. You should
have twice the amount of corn mixture to meat in each tamale.

Wrap the corn husks to form a parcel, adding extra leaves if necessary (the mixture
should be completely enclosed). Secure with cooking twine or husk strips.

Place the tamales in a bamboo steamer and steam them for around 40 minutes or
until firm. Serve still encased in the corn husks, but remove the husks before eating.

Makes around 8 tamales

TAMALES DULCES
· sweet tamales ·

For the filling:

250 g (9 oz) fresh, hulled strawberries,
 or 120 g (4½ oz/¾ cup) pineapple
 pieces
55 g (2 oz/¼ cup) sugar
1 teaspoon lemon juice
60 ml (2 fl oz/¼ cup) water

For the tamale wrapping:

24–30 dried corn husks *
cooking twine or strips of corn husk

For the tamale dough:

10 corn cobs or 750 g (1 lb 11 oz/
 3¾ cups) corn kernels
30 g (1 oz/¼ cup) powdered coconut
 cream powder (to make coconut
 tamales)
300 g (10½ oz) lard or butter
110 g (4 oz/½ cup) sugar
1 teaspoon salt
20 g (¾ oz) masa harina for tamales **

* Available from specialist delicatessens.

** Masa harina is a special flour made from corn, available at specialty delicatessens. If 'tamale' masa harina is not available, just use regular masa harina.

For the filling, place all the ingredients in a small saucepan over a medium heat. Bring gently to the boil, and then reduce the heat to low and allow to simmer until the fruit has softened and the mixture is bubbly. Remove from the heat and set aside to cool.

To prepare the dough, if using corn cobs, remove the kernels using a sharp knife.

In a bowl, mix together the corn kernels with the coconut cream powder (if making coconut tamales), lard, sugar and salt. Process with a hand-held blender until almost completely puréed.

Add the masa harina and mix well using a wooden spoon. The mixture should be the consistency of toothpaste. Set aside.

To assemble the tamales, take 2 or 3 corn husks and shape them together like the hull of a canoe. Spread a large tablespoon of the corn mixture into the corn husk 'canoe', then a tablespoon of the puréed fruit and finish with another tablespoon of corn mixture.

Wrap the overlapping corn husks to form a parcel, adding extra leaves if necessary. Secure with cooking twine or strips of corn husk.

Place the tamales in a bamboo steamer and steam for about 40 minutes. Serve when cooled in the husks, but remove the husks before eating.

Makes around 8 tamales

QUESADILLAS CON QUESO Y FLOR DE CALABAZA

.zucchini blossom & cheese. quesadillas

1 tablespoon vegetable oil
½ fresh jalapeño, seeded and finely chopped
2 large ripe tomatoes, peeled and finely chopped
1 tablespoon finely chopped white onion
4 basil leaves, chopped
300 g (10½ oz) zucchini (courgette) blossoms, chopped
125 g (4½ oz) queso fresco or low-salt feta, grated
300 g (10½ oz) fresh masa dough for tortillas (see page 72)
salsa of your choice to serve

Heat the vegetable oil in a saucepan over a medium heat. Add the chilli, tomatoes, onion and basil. Cover the pan and cook over a low heat for about 15 minutes or until the tomatoes have broken down and turned into a thick sauce. Remove from the heat.

Add the zucchini blossoms and cheese to the hot sauce and set aside.

Using portions of masa dough the size of a lime, form tortillas using a tortilla press or by rolling the dough between 2 pieces of baking paper with a rolling pin until very thin.

Place a tablespoon of the quesadilla filling in the centre of each raw tortilla. Fold the tortilla over and seal the edges by pressing with your fingertips. Cook the quesadilla in an oiled frying pan over a medium heat for 3–4 minutes on each side and serve immediately with the salsa of your choice.

Makes 8 quesadillas

Variation: For *quesadillas con queso y hongos* (mushroom quesadillas), replace the zucchini blossoms with 300 g (10½ oz) wild mushrooms that have been chopped and sautéed in 30 g (1 oz) butter for about 10 minutes.

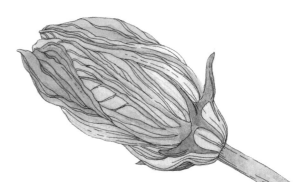

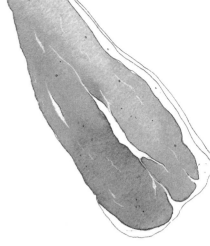

QUESADILLAS SINCRONIZADAS

. Serrano ham & cheese .
quesadillas

For the flour tortillas:

300 g (10½ oz/2 cups) plain (all-purpose)
    flour
2 tablespoons olive oil or lard, plus extra
    for frying
½ teaspoon salt
125 ml (4 fl oz/½ cup) warm water

For the filling:
12 slices Serrano ham
12 slices sharp cheese, such as gruyère

For the avocado mash:

2 avocados
40 g (1½ oz/¼ cup) finely chopped
    red onion
½ ripe tomato, finely chopped
¼ bunch of coriander (cilantro) leaves,
    chopped
iceberg lettuce leaves, whole
3 radishes, thinly sliced

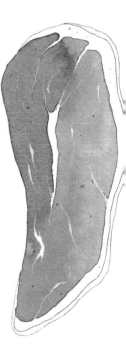

If making fresh tortillas (you can save time by using store-bought tortillas if you wish), place the flour in a large bowl. Add the olive oil or lard and combine with clean fingertips until a sand-like consistency is achieved.

Dissolve the salt in the warm water and add this to the flour. Work the dough with your hands, adding extra water if needed to form a smooth, non-sticky dough that is easy to handle.

Divide into 6 equal portions. Form tortillas using a tortilla press or by rolling the dough between 2 sheets of baking paper with a rolling pin until very thin. Cook the tortillas in a lightly oiled frying pan over a high heat for about 1 minute on each side. Keep the tortillas warm by wrapping them in a clean tea towel (dish towel).

To assemble a quesadilla, top 1 tortilla with a slice or two of ham, a slice or two of cheese and then top with another tortilla. Make the remaining quesadillas in this way until all your ingredients have been used. Set aside.

For the avocado mash, using a fork, mash the flesh of the avocados with the onion, tomato and coriander. Add salt to taste.

To serve, pile 2 tablespoons of the mash on a lettuce leaf and top with the radish slices. Arrange this lettuce and avocado cup in the centre of each individual plate.

To finish making the quesadillas, cook them in a lightly oiled frying pan over a medium–high heat, one at a time, for about 3–5 minutes on each side or until the cheese begins to melt and the tortillas are slightly toasted. Cut each quesadilla into quarters and arrange them around the avocado and lettuce cups.

Makes 6 quesadillas

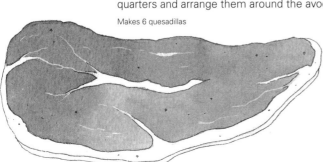

QUESADILLAS CON CHORIZO DE TOLUCA

·Toluca chorizo quesadillas·

The chorizo used in this recipe is very special and unique to the town of Toluca, a colourful place about 65 km (40 miles) southwest of Mexico City. When Abuelo travelled to Acapulco with his family for a vacation, he would always stop in Toluca to buy fresh produce such as queso fresco, freshly baked Mexican bread and this special chorizo.

500 g (1 lb 2 oz) pork shoulder, minced (ground)
175 g (6 oz) lard
1 dried ancho chilli
2 dried pasilla chillies
½ white onion, finely chopped
125 ml (4 fl oz/½ cup) white vinegar
3 garlic cloves
1 teaspoon ground cumin
1 teaspoon ground cloves
1 teaspoon freshly ground black pepper

1 teaspoon ground cinnamon
1 teaspoon ground coriander
1 teaspoon dried oregano
20 g (¾ oz) sweet paprika
2 teaspoons salt
1 tablespoon vegetable oil for frying
300 g (10½ oz) fresh masa dough for tortillas (see page 72)
300 g (10½ oz) queso fresco or low-salt feta, grated
salsa of your choice to serve

Combine the pork with the lard in a deep bowl and set aside.

Dry-roast the chillies in a frying pan over a medium–high heat for a few minutes until they are soft and have started to release their oils. Remove the stems, seeds and membranes. Soak the chillies in hot water for 20 minutes.

Drain the chillies and place them in a food processor or blender along with the remaining ingredients, except the vegetable oil, dough and queso fresco. Process until smooth. Add the chilli mixture to the pork and, using your hands, work the mixture to combine. (At this point you can refrigerate or even freeze the pork until needed.)

Once ready to use, fry the chorizo mixture in the oil in a frying pan over a medium–high heat for about 5 minutes or until the chorizo is cooked through. Set aside.

Using portions of masa dough the size of a lime, form tortillas using a tortilla press or by rolling the dough between 2 pieces of baking paper with a rolling pin until very thin.

Place 1 tablespoon of the cooked chorizo in the centre of each raw tortilla. Add a little queso fresco. Fold the tortilla over and seal the edges by pressing with your fingertips. Cook the quesadillas in an oiled frying pan over a medium heat for about 3–4 minutes on each side and serve immediately with a salsa of your choice.

Makes around 8 quesadillas

TOLUCA
DE LERDO

TORTAS

TELERAS

MEDIAS NOCHES

BOLILLOS

PAMBAZOS

SALSAS

MEXICAN SANDWICHES

Breadmaking has been a tradition in my family for generations. My Abuelo's father, Roberto, was a baker, as well as running a successful seafood restaurant in Alvarado. Abuelo would help make the bread with his father and stepmother, also selling the bread and other baked goods from door to door around the streets of his home town. Abuelo could knead dough for hours!

Tortas are Mexican sandwiches made from a variety of lovely bread rolls, many of which my Abuelo would bake and sell as a young man. The following recipes range from lovely light buns to more substantial rolls filled with wonderful melt-in-your-mouth meats. *Torta* street stands are very common in Mexico – they are the perfect quick snack for the office worker.

·TELERAS·

· savoury buns ·

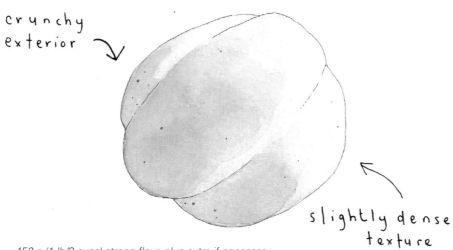

crunchy
exterior

slightly dense
texture

450 g (1 lb/3 cups) strong flour, plus extra if necessary
14 g (½ oz) dried yeast
1 tablespoon sugar
1¼ teaspoons salt
250 ml (8½ fl oz/1 cup) water

Sift the flour directly onto a work surface. Spread the flour out a little and add the dried yeast, sugar and salt. Mix thoroughly with your hands, adding the water a little at a time, bringing the mixture together and working the dough until all the water is added. The dough's texture should be a little dry.

Keep working the dough, kneading for a few minutes until it is pliable, smooth and does not stick to the work surface or to your hands.

Shape the dough into a ball, place it in a greased bowl, cover with a clean tea towel (dish towel) and leave to rest in a warm spot.

Preheat the oven to 180°C (350°F).

Once the dough has doubled in size, after about 1 hour, cut it into 8 portions and shape the teleras into log shapes. With both hands, flatten the sides a little. The centre will bulge, but that's okay. This will give the telera its original shape when cooked.

Place the teleras on an oiled baking tray and bake them in the oven for 20–25 minutes or until golden. Allow them to cool on a wire rack before adding the fillings (see opposite page for suggestions).

Makes 8 buns

FILLINGS
FOR TELERAS

chipotle chilli, chicken breast,
lettuce, avocado slices,
topped with mayonnaise

borlotti (cranberry) beans, mozzarella
cheese melted & topped with
salsa roja (page 51)

Serrano ham, lettuce, thinly sliced
red onion, Monterey Jack cheese,
sliced jalapeño & sliced tomato

MEDIAS NOCHES

· 'midnights' ·

slightly
sweet

super light
& fluffy

170 ml (5½ fl oz/⅔ cup) milk
115 g (4 oz/½ cup) caster (superfine)
  sugar, plus an extra ½ teaspoon
1 teaspoon salt
150 g (5½ oz) butter, melted
14 g (½ oz) dried yeast

60 ml (2 fl oz/¼ cup) warm water
4 eggs, lightly beaten, plus 1 extra beaten
  egg for glazing
550 g (1 lb 3 oz/3⅔ cups) strong flour

In a large bowl mix the milk, sugar, salt and melted butter for about 2–3 minutes until the sugar has dissolved.

Mix the dried yeast into the warm water, add the extra ½ teaspoon sugar and set aside for 5 minutes until the yeast starts to bubble. Once bubbly, mix in the 4 beaten eggs.

Add half the flour to the egg–yeast mixture and combine until the flour is incorporated. Add the rest of the flour, mixing with your hands, until the dough holds its shape and is easy to knead. Knead the dough for about 15 minutes until it is elastic and air bubbles can be seen under the surface. Place the dough in a greased bowl, covered with a clean tea towel (dish towel), and place in a warm spot for 2 hours or until the dough has doubled in size.

Punch the dough and cut it in half, and then each half in half again, and so on until you end up with 30 pieces of dough (each about the size of an apricot). Roll each ball between the palms of your hands to give it the shape of a sausage about 1½ cm (½ in) across and 5 cm (2 in) long.

Preheat the oven to 200°C (400°F). Place the dough on a baking tray, leaving room between the pieces to allow rising. Cover the tray with a clean tea towel and leave in a warm spot for about 1 hour. They should double in size. Don't worry if the buns stick to each other – they can be pulled apart once they are cooked.

Brush the tops of the buns with the beaten egg and bake in the oven for 5–6 minutes. Your medias noches should look golden and glossy but not brown. Let them rest for a minute, then allow to cool completely on a wire rack.

Gently pull apart the medias noches if they have stuck together. Store them in an airtight container until ready to eat. They will keep for a couple of days. (See opposite page for filling suggestions.)

Makes 30 buns

FILLINGS FOR MEDIAS NOCHES

Media noche literally means 'midnight' and these are so named because people tend to eat them after a night out or as a midnight snack. The light and fluffy texture and slight sweetness of these bread rolls work really well with the savoury fillings.

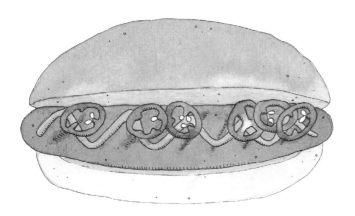

American frankfurt sausage, American mustard & sliced ← jalapeño chilli

Monterey Jack cheese, Serrano ham & sliced jalapeño chilli

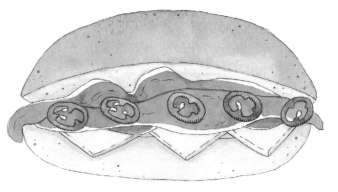

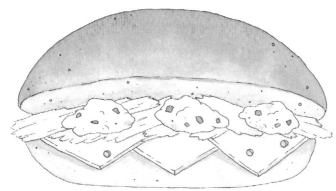

gruyère cheese, shredded chicken & tartare sauce

· BOLILLOS ·

· light-as-a-feather buns ·

super crunchy ↓

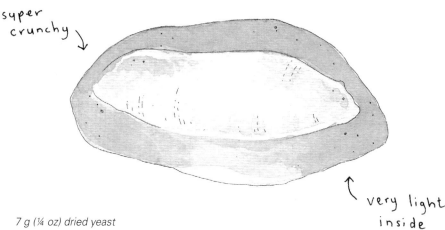

↑ very light inside

7 g (¼ oz) dried yeast
310 ml (10½ fl oz/1¼ cup) warm water
300 g (10½ oz/2 cups) strong flour
2 teaspoons sugar
½ teaspoon salt

Dissolve the yeast in 60 ml (2 fl oz/¼ cup) of the warm water and rest for 5 minutes or until it bubbles.

Place the flour in a large bowl. Add the dissolved yeast, sugar, salt and the remaining warm water, mixing to combine. The dough should be a little sticky and moist.

Knead the dough on a lightly floured surface for 10 minutes or until smooth and elastic. Shape the dough into a ball, place in a greased bowl, cover with a clean tea towel (dish towel) and rest in a warm spot for around 2 hours, or until doubled in size.

Punch the dough and cut it in half, and then each half in half again, and then again until you end up with 8 pieces of dough. Shape each piece into a rectangle. Fold the long edges over by 1 cm (½ in) towards the middle of the rectangle. Then, using a rolling pin, roll out very slightly so the edges are squashed down a bit.

Preheat the oven to 180°C (350°F).

Place the bolillos on a greased baking tray and allow them to rest again, covered with a tea towel, for a further hour or until doubled in size.

Bake in the oven for 20 minutes or until just golden. The outside should be crusty and the inside soft. Traditionally served as a side bread with soup, you can also fill them with your favourite sandwich filling.

Makes 8 buns

PAMBAZOS

· little buns ·

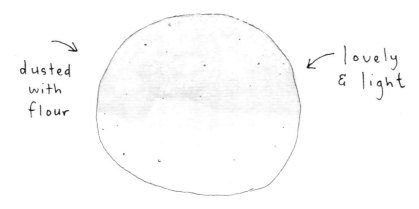

dusted with flour

lovely & light

These are lovely light buns that are served as finger food on special occasions. Traditional fillings include *papas con chorizo* (chorizo and potatoes) and pulled pork, beef or chicken. See the recipes on pages 48–9.

7 g (¼ oz) dried yeast
170 ml (5½ fl oz/⅔ cup) warm water
500 g (1 lb 2 oz/3⅓ cups) strong flour
1 tablespoon sugar
1 teaspoon salt
100 g (3½ oz) lard, at room temperature

Dissolve the yeast in a little of the warm water and rest for 5 minutes or until it bubbles. Add the remaining water. Set aside.

Place the flour in a large bowl with the sugar and salt and combine. Using your hands, mix in the softened lard and yeast–water mixture. Add a little more water if necessary to form a smooth, pliable dough.

Knead the dough on a lightly floured surface for about 15 minutes or until elastic and glossy. Shape the dough into a ball, place in a greased bowl, cover with a clean tea towel (dish towel) and leave to rest in a warm place for around 2 hours or until doubled in size.

Punch the dough down and knead lightly.

Cut the dough into 20 even-sized pieces and shape into walnut-sized balls. Roll out the balls slightly with a rolling pin, shaping them into elongated circles. Place on a baking tray lined with baking paper, cover with a tea towel and allow to rest for a further hour.

Preheat the oven to 180°C (350°F). Bake the pambazos for 15 minutes or until golden.

Your pambazos are ready to be filled with a range of fillings (see pages 48–9).

Makes around 20

. FILLINGS .

CARNE DE PUERCO CON SALSA DE AGUACATE
. pulled pork & . avocado salsa

300 g (10½ oz) pork leg cut into
    3 cm (1¼ in) pieces
500 ml (17 fl oz/2 cups) water
3 pink peppercorns
½ white onion, chopped
2 garlic cloves
1 teaspoon salt
1 bay leaf
1 teaspoon dried marjoram
1 tablespoon white vinegar
4 Pambazos (page 47)
Salsa de aguacate (page 50)

Place all the ingredients, except the
pambazos and salsa, in a saucepan
over a medium heat. Bring to the
boil then reduce the heat to low and
simmer for 45 minutes or until the
pork is very tender.

Remove the pork from the stock
and shred using 2 forks.

Fill the pambazos while the meat is still
hot. Smother the meat with salsa de
aguacate and serve.

Makes 4

PAPAS CON CHORIZO Y SALSA VERDE
. potato, chorizo . & green sauce

1 tablespoon lard or olive oil
2 chorizo sausages, diced into
    1 cm (½ in) cubes
1 onion, finely chopped
3 waxy potatoes, cut into
    1 cm (½ in) cubes
500 ml (17 fl oz/2 cups) tomato passata
    (puréed tomatoes)
4 tinned chipotle chillies in escabeche
    (brine), cut into strips
15 g (½ oz/¼ cup) chopped coriander
    (cilantro) leaves
4 Pambazos (page 47)
Salsa verde (page 50)

In a heavy frying pan, heat the lard over
a medium–high heat and fry the chorizo
with the onion for a few minutes. When
the onion is translucent, add the potato
and fry for a further 2 minutes.

Add the tomato passata, chipotle,
coriander and salt to taste. Cover
and allow to simmer over a low heat
for 10 minutes or until the potatoes
are cooked.

Fill the pambazos with the mixture
while still hot and serve with the
salsa verde.

Makes 4

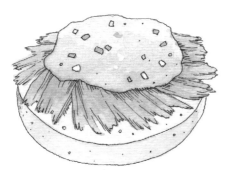

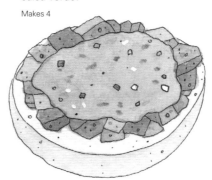

· FILLINGS ·

CARNE DE RES Y SALSA DE FRIJOLES
· pulled beef in · bean sauce

300 g (10½ oz) shin beef cut into
   3 cm (1¼ in) pieces
500 ml (17 fl oz/2 cups) water
3 pink peppercorns
½ white onion, chopped
2 garlic cloves
1 teaspoon salt
1 bay leaf
1 tablespoon white vinegar
4 Pambazos (page 47)
Salsa de frijol (page 51)

Place all the ingredients, except the
pambazos and salsa, in a saucepan
over a medium heat. Bring to the
boil then reduce the heat to low and
simmer for 45 minutes or until the beef
is very tender.

Remove the beef from the stock
and shred using 2 forks.

Fill the pambazos while the meat is still
hot. Smother the meat with salsa de
frijol and serve.

Makes 4

POLLO CON SALSA ROJA
· pulled chicken · in red sauce

1 large skinless, boneless chicken
   breast (approximately 200 g/7 oz)
500 ml (17 fl oz/2 cups) water
3 pink peppercorns
½ white onion, chopped
2 garlic cloves
1 teaspoon salt
1 bay leaf
1 tablespoon white vinegar
4 Pambazos (page 47)
Salsa roja (page 51)

Place all the ingredients, except the
pambazos and salsa, in a saucepan
over a medium heat. Bring to the
boil and then reduce the heat to low,
simmering for 30 minutes or until the
chicken is very tender.

Remove the chicken from the stock
and shred using 2 forks.

Fill the pambazos while the meat is
still hot. Smother the chicken with the
salsa roja and serve.

Makes 4

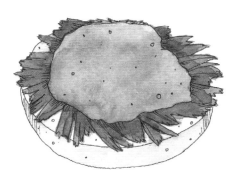

· SALSAS ·

SALSA VERDE
· green sauce ·

250 ml (8½ fl oz/1 cup) water
4 green chillies such as jalapeños
¼ white onion, roughly chopped
200 g (7 oz) fresh or tinned peeled tomatillos
½ bunch of coriander (cilantro)
juice of ½ lime

In a small saucepan over a medium heat, combine half the water, the chillies, onion and tomatillos. Bring to the boil and then turn off the heat. Allow to cool slightly.

Transfer the mixture to a blender along with the remaining ingredients and process until the mixture is smooth.

Store in the refrigerator for up to 3 weeks.

Makes 375 g (13 oz/1½ cups) salsa

SALSA DE AGUACATE
· avocado sauce ·

2 avocados
250 g (9 oz/1 cup) Salsa verde (see left)
7 g (¼ oz/¼ cup) coriander (cilantro) leaves, chopped

Scoop the flesh of the avocados into a bowl. Mix in the salsa verde using a fork until combined.

Mix through the coriander. The sauce should be nice and chunky. It is best served immediately.

Makes 375 g (13 oz/1½ cups) salsa

· SALSAS ·

SALSA DE FRIJOL
· bean sauce ·

*2 avocado tree leaves ***
1 green chilli, e.g. jalapeño
1 garlic clove
400 g (14 oz) tin borlotti (cranberry)
  beans, drained

* 5 fresh basil leaves may be substituted.

Heat the avocado leaves over an open flame (e.g. a gas burner) until they release their oil – be careful not to burn them. Skip this step if you are using basil instead.

Place the leaves in a food processor or blender along with the chilli, garlic and beans. Process and add just enough water to give the mixture a salsa consistency. Season to taste. It is best served immediately.

Makes 250 g (9 oz/1 cup) salsa

SALSA ROJA
· red sauce ·

125 ml (4 fl oz/½ cup) water
2 whole tomatoes
1 red chilli, roughly chopped
¼ white onion
7 g (¼ oz/¼ cup) coriander (cilantro)
  leaves
½ teaspoon salt

Place all the ingredients, except the salt, in a small saucepan over a high heat. Bring to the boil, reduce the heat to low and then simmer for 5 minutes.

Remove the tomatoes, keeping the water in the pot. Carefully remove the skin from the tomatoes.

Place all the ingredients, including the water and salt, into a blender and process until the sauce is smooth. Store in the refrigerator for up to 3 weeks.

Makes 375 g (13 oz/1½ cups) salsa

¡NIEVES!

· LIMÓN ·   · PIÑA ·

· SANDÍA ·   · ELOTE ·

· SAPOTE NEGRO ·

· TAMARINDO ·

SORBETS + GELATO

Nieves are very similar to Italian gelatos and sorbets but what makes them uniquely Mexican is the range of flavours, some of them based on exotic fruits like black and red sapote, originally only found in Latin American countries.

Mobile *nieve* and *helado* (ice cream) vendors are everywhere in Mexico City, tempting passersby with the colourful icy treats in their quirky carts.

· LIMÓN ·
· lime sorbet ·

1 litre (34 fl oz/4 cups) water
350 g (12½ oz) sugar
zest and juice of 5 limes
green food colouring (optional)

Place the water and the sugar in a deep saucepan. Bring to the boil over a medium heat, stirring to dissolve the sugar. Bring the temperature to just over 100°C (212°F) on a candy thermometer so it forms a syrup. Remove from the heat and allow to cool completely.

Add the lime zest, juice and food colouring, if using, to the cooled syrup, mixing until well combined.

For best results, use an ice-cream maker:

Pour the mixture into a bowl and cover tightly with foil. Place in the freezer for around 1 hour or until quite cold but not yet freezing.

Place the mixture in your ice-cream maker and follow the manufacturer's instructions.

If you don't have an ice-cream maker:

Pour the mixture into a tray and place in the freezer for at least 4 hours. Transfer to a bowl and, using a hand-held blender, blend the semi-frozen sorbet for 1–2 minutes.

Pour the mixture back into the freezer tray and freeze for another 2 hours. Repeat the process 2–3 more times or until the frozen mixture has reached sorbet consistency. Freeze overnight.

Makes 1 litre (34 fl oz/4 cups)

· TAMARINDO ·
· tamarind sorbet ·

300 g (10½ oz) sugar
50 g (1¾ oz) glucose powder
650 ml (22 fl oz) water
150 g (5½ oz) tamarind paste, plus an
extra tablespoon if you like it tangy

Place all the ingredients, except the tamarind paste, in a saucepan. Bring to the boil over a medium heat, stirring to dissolve the sugar. Bring the temperature to just over 100°C (212°F) on a candy thermometer so it forms a syrup.

Remove from the heat and allow to cool completely. Add the tamarind paste and mix until well combined.

For best results, use an ice-cream maker:

Pour the mixture into a bowl and cover tightly with foil. Place in the freezer for around 1 hour or until quite cold but not yet freezing.

Place the mixture in your ice-cream maker and follow the manufacturer's instructions. Halfway through the churning process, add the extra tablespoon of tamarind paste, if using – this will give little bursts of sourness to your sorbet, which works brilliantly with the sorbet's sweetness.

If you don't have an ice-cream maker:

Pour the mixture into a tray and place in the freezer for at least 4 hours. Transfer to a bowl and, using a hand-held blender, blend the semi-frozen sorbet for 1–2 minutes.

Pour the mixture back into the freezer tray and freeze for another 2 hours. Repeat the process 2–3 more times or until the frozen mixture has reached sorbet consistency. At this point, add the extra tablespoon of tamarind paste, if using. Freeze overnight.

Makes 1 litre (34 fl oz/4 cups)

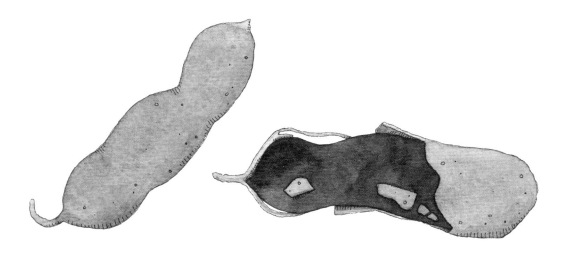

· SANDÍA ·
· watermelon gelato ·

500 g (1 lb 2 oz) watermelon flesh,
   cut into rough chunks with seeds
   removed, plus extra to serve
250 g (9 oz/2 cups) icing (confectioners') sugar
juice of 1 lemon
350 ml (12 fl oz) thick (double/heavy) cream
spearmint leaves to garnish (optional)

Place the watermelon in a blender and process until smooth. Add the icing sugar and lemon juice and blend again. You can do this in batches.

If you have an ice-cream maker:

Pour the mixture into a bowl and cover tightly with foil. Place in the freezer for around 1 hour or until quite cold but not yet freezing. Meanwhile, beat the cream for a few minutes until thickened. Add the cream to the cold watermelon mixture.

Place the mixture in your ice-cream maker and follow the manufacturer's instructions.

If you don't have an ice-cream maker:

Place the watermelon mixture in the freezer for around 1 hour. Beat the cream for a few minutes until thickened, then add to the cold watermelon mixture. Pour the mixture into a tray and place in the freezer for at least 4 hours. Transfer to a bowl and, using a hand-held blender, blend the semi-frozen gelato for 1–2 minutes. Pour the mixture back into the tray and freeze for another 2 hours.

Repeat the process 2–3 more times or until the frozen mixture has reached gelato consistency. Freeze overnight.

Serve garnished with watermelon pieces and some spearmint leaves, if desired.

Makes 1 litre (34 fl oz/4 cups)

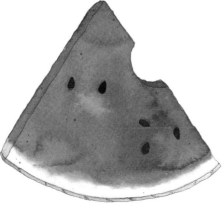

· PIÑA ·

· pineapple sorbet ·

800 g (1 lb 12 oz) fresh pineapple,
  cored and cut into chunks (tinned
  unsweetened pineapple pieces can also
  be used), plus extra pieces to garnish
115 g (4 oz/½ cup) muscovado sugar
125 ml (4 fl oz/½ cup) agave syrup*
1 teaspoon vanilla bean paste
mint leaves to garnish (optional)

* Available in the specialty food aisle of supermarkets
or delicatessens.

Place all the ingredients, except the mint leaves, in a blender or food processor and blend for 1–2 minutes or until smooth. You can do this in batches if you need to.

If you have an ice-cream maker:

Pour the mixture into a bowl and cover tightly with foil. Place in the freezer for around 1 hour or until quite cold but not yet freezing.

Place the mixture in your ice-cream maker and follow the manufacturer's instructions.

If you don't have an ice-cream maker:

Pour the mixture into a bowl and cover tightly with foil. Place in the freezer for about 4 hours or until partially frozen.

Scrape the pineapple mixture into a blender or food processor and blend for 1–2 minutes. Pour it back into the bowl, cover and return to the freezer. Repeat the beating and freezing process 2–3 times or until the frozen mixture reaches a sorbet consistency.

Freeze overnight. Serve with small chunks of fresh pineapple and mint leaves, if desired.

Makes 1.5 litres (51 fl oz/6 cups)

· ELOTE ·
· sweetcorn gelato ·

1 egg
2 egg yolks
230 g (8 oz/1 cup) muscovado sugar
500 ml (17 fl oz/2 cups) milk
300 ml (10 fl oz) thick (double/heavy)
  cream

800 g (1 lb 12 oz/4 cups) fresh corn
  kernels
¼ teaspoon salt
1 teaspoon vanilla bean paste or the
  seeds from 1 vanilla bean
corn husks to serve

Using an electric mixer, cream the egg, egg yolks and sugar together until pale.

Place the milk, cream, corn kernels, salt and vanilla in a saucepan over a low heat. Simmer gently for 10 minutes or until the corn is tender. Remove from the heat.

Process the milk mixture in a blender until smooth and then return to the saucepan over a low heat. Pour a little of the milk mixture into the egg mixture and whisk until well combined. Pour the egg mixture into the remaining milk mixture and combine.

Strain the mixture into a bowl through a sieve, pressing down with the back of a spoon to extract as much of the liquid as possible. Pour back into the saucepan and bring to a gentle simmer over a low heat for about 15 minutes or until the mixture has thickened slightly. Do not allow to boil. Cool completely.

If you have an ice-cream maker:

Pour the mixture into a bowl and cover tightly with foil. Place in the freezer for around 1 hour or until quite cold but not yet freezing.

Place the mixture in your ice-cream maker and follow the manufacturer's instructions.

If you don't have an ice-cream maker:

Pour the mixture into a bowl and cover tightly with foil. Place in the freezer for about 4 hours or until partially frozen.

Using a hand-held blender, blend for 1–2 minutes. Freeze the mixture again for 2 hours. Repeat the beating and freezing process a couple more times or until the mixture reaches gelato consistency.

Serve in bowls lined with dried corn husk leaves.

Makes 1.5 litres (51 fl oz/6 cups)

SAPOTE NEGRO
· black sapote sorbet ·

Black sapote is a type of persimmon native to Mexico. It looks a little like an unripe tomato but has dark brown flesh with the taste and texture of chocolate pudding. Black sapotes were my Abuelo's all-time favourite fruit.

350 g (12½ oz) sugar
1 litre (34 fl oz/4 cups) water
juice of ½ lime
juice of 1 orange
3 fresh black sapotes, flesh scooped out
  and seeds removed

Place the sugar and water in a deep saucepan over a medium heat and bring to the boil. Reduce the heat to low and simmer for around 10 minutes or until it starts to thicken into a syrup. Allow to cool slightly.

Place the sugar syrup, lime juice, orange juice and sapote flesh in a food processor and process until smooth. Allow to cool completely.

If you have an ice-cream maker:

Pour the mixture into a bowl and cover tightly with foil. Place in the freezer for around 1 hour or until quite cold but not yet freezing.

Place the mixture in your ice-cream maker and follow the manufacturer's instructions.

If you don't have an ice-cream maker:

Pour the mixture into a bowl and cover tightly with foil. Place in the freezer for about 4 hours or until partially frozen.

Using a hand-held blender, blend for 1–2 minutes. Freeze the mixture again for 2 hours. Repeat the beating and freezing process a couple more times or until the mixture reaches sorbet consistency.

Freeze overnight.

Makes 1.5 litres (51 fl oz/6 cups)

CIUDAD DE
MÉXICO

CATEDRAL METROPOLITANA

MEXICO CITY

At the age of twenty-five Abuelo was well on his way to becoming a doctor after being accepted into the medical program at the Universidad Nacional Autónoma de México. He returned to Alvarado regularly to help my great grandfather and, on one of those visits, he approached my Abuela's parents to ask for permission to date their daughter.

According to my mum, even though Abuelo had fallen head over heels in love with Abuela years prior, it was not until he returned to Alvarado as a young medical student that he felt he could offer her a future. They were married in the same year of his graduation.

I have many fond memories of staying with Abuelo and Abuela in their beautiful home in Mexico City. We would take many trips to the *hipódromo* (race course) to watch Abuelo's horses run. Many days were also spent wandering the amazing arts and crafts markets in the city.

Abuelo would often take us to a very famous restaurant in Mexico City called Arroyo. I have vivid memories of the wonderful food we had there. The following recipes are a collection reminiscent of the typical feast we enjoyed at Arroyo. Of course, we kids would not partake in the tequila!

TEQUILA CON LIMÓN Y SANGRITA

·tequila with lime & sangrita·

The Arroyo restaurant experience would start with tequila served in salt-rimmed *caballitos* (small shot glasses), lime wedges and a small glass of sangrita (a spicy contrast to the strong flavour of tequila). Sangrita is not to be confused with sangría!

For the sangrita:

4 ripe tomatoes
½ small white onion, thinly sliced
juice of 1 orange
juice of 1 lime
1 jalapeño, seeded and membrane
  removed, thinly sliced
5 drops of worcestershire sauce

To serve:

good-quality tequila
fresh lime
salt

Cut the tomatoes into quarters and squeeze them over a colander, capturing the juices in a bowl. Set the juice aside.

Place the onion and orange and lime juices in another bowl and macerate for about 30 minutes.

Pour the onion-infused juice into the tomato juice (discard the onion slices) and add the remaining ingredients, mixing well. Cover with plastic wrap and refrigerate for several hours or overnight.

Strain the sangrita into a clean pitcher (discard the chilli slices) and serve while still cold in a tequila glass. Pour a shot of tequila into a separate glass. To drink, have a sip of tequila, a sip of sangrita, a suck of lime and a lick of salt.

Serve with salty Chicharrón (page 71) dipped in the salsa of your choice.

Makes about 500 ml (17 fl oz/2 cups)

Variation: *Cóctel vampiro* (vampire tequila) can be made by mixing equal parts of tequila and sangrita. Serve very cold in a salt-rimmed cocktail glass.

MICHELADAS
·beer & lime cocktail·

This is a very Mexican (and tasty) way of drinking beer.

250 ml (8½ fl oz/1 cup) lager beer
2 tablespoons lime juice
1 teaspoon worcestershire sauce
¼ teaspoon Tabasco sauce
¼ teaspoon of Maggi seasoning sauce
crushed ice

Place a cold beer glass and the beer in the freezer for 20 minutes prior to preparing.

Place the lime juice, worcestershire sauce, Tabasco sauce and seasoning sauce in the beer glass. Add the ice and mix with a long spoon.

Carefully pour in the beer. Serve with Cacahuates enchilados (page 27).

Serves 1

Option: The glass can be rimmed with lime juice and dipped in salt before adding the ingredients.

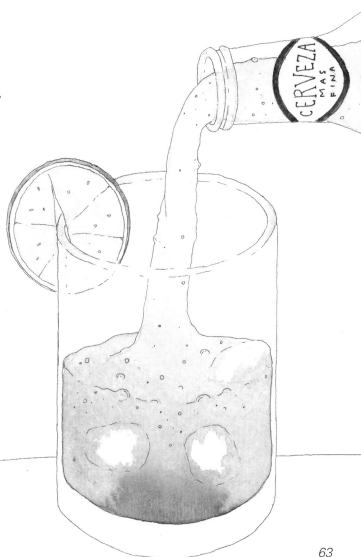

CÓCTEL MARGARITA

· margarita ·

A favourite of my mum's, this is the typical ladies' tequila cocktail. There are many versions out there but this one is the real thing. In my mum's words, 'one margarita is guaranteed to transport you to a feeling of floating over grassy, flowery meadows!'

salt to rim glass
juice of ½ lime
30 ml (1 fl oz) tequila
15 ml (½ fl oz) curacao liqueur
juice of ½ orange
75 g (2¾ oz/½ cup) crushed ice
lime slices to serve

Spread some salt on a side plate. Rub the rims of 2 cocktail glasses with lime juice. Turn the glasses upside down and dip the rims in the salt, using a circular motion.

Mix all the ingredients in a cocktail shaker and shake vigorously for about 5 seconds. Strain into the glasses and serve with a slice of lime on the edge of each glass.

Serves 2

Variation: Frozen margaritas can be made using the same ingredients, but leave the ice out and the lime and orange juices should be frozen (use ice cube trays for this).

Place all the ingredients in a blender and process for 3–5 seconds. Serve the cocktail immediately in salt-rimmed glasses.

TORITOS DE FRUTAS

· 'bull by the horns' cocktail ·

This delicious drink originates from Veracruz but is very popular throughout Mexico. It is traditionally made from cane-based alcohol and flavoured with natural fruits. Its name dates back to when local workers spent very long working days cutting sugar cane. They prepared this fruit drink so they felt as strong as *toros* (bulls) and would be able to get through the day's work.

355 ml (12 fl oz) evaporated milk
395 ml (13½ fl oz) condensed milk
500 ml (17 fl oz/2 cups) white rum
250 g (9 oz) strawberries, mango,
*   custard-apple, guava or pineapple pieces*
135 g (5 oz/1 cup) ice cubes

Place all the ingredients in a blender and process until smooth. Serve in tall glasses with a straw.

Serves 6

KNOW YOUR TEQUILAS

Tequila is a spirit made from the distilled sap of the blue agave plant, grown almost exclusively in the highlands of Jalisco state in central Mexico. Tequila, as we know it today, was first made using distilling techniques brought to Mexico by the Spanish conquistadors shortly after their arrival in the early 1500s.

BLANCO

Blanco tequila is the original and most common form of tequila. It is 'un-aged' (under 60 days old) and it is considered to be tastier than other highly refined varieties. It is clear in colour, hence its name, which translates to 'white' tequila.

The taste varies depending on where the agaves are grown. Highland styles are known for their brighter, acidic and peppery tones. Lowland styles are fruitier and spicier.

REPOSADO

Reposado tequila is aged from 2 months up to a year, often in large oak casks or smaller barrels. Its taste is more complex and rich than blanco tequila, and its colour is golden, darkening with time. The wood of the barrel affects the flavour.

Gran reposado is the unofficial name for reposados that are aged even longer than usual.

To be classified as tequila, it must be made from at least 51 per cent Weber Blue agave. High-quality tequilas are 100 per cent blue agave. If it's not 100 per cent agave, then it is called a *mixto*. Contrary to popular belief, bottles of tequila never contain a worm. The 'worm' (larvae of the agave snout weevil) is only ever found in bottles of mezcal, another spirit made from agave, produced using a different method from that used for tequila, with a more smoky taste.

AÑEJO

EXTRA AÑEJO

Añejo tequila is aged for at least 1 year, and has a lovely amber colour. Many añejos become quite dark and the influence of the wood is greater than in reposado.

Extra añejo tequila is aged for more than 3 years, and therefore has a much darker, mahogany colour.

It is the most complex and smooth form of tequila. Tequila is considered to be at its best at 4 or 5 years, but may be aged for up to 10 years.

ENSALADA
DE NOPALES

·young cactus salad·

Nopal (also known as 'prickly pear') is commonly used in
Mexican cooking and can be eaten cooked or raw. When cooked, nopal has
a texture and taste similar to cooked green capsicum (bell pepper).

4 nopales (young cactus leaves)*
½ teaspoon salt
1 jalapeño, seeded and sliced
¼ white onion, thinly sliced
4 coriander (cilantro) sprigs, chopped
½ teaspoon dried oregano
60 ml (2 fl oz/¼ cup) white vinegar
60 ml (2 fl oz/¼ cup) extra-virgin
  olive oil
75 g (2¾ oz/½ cup) grated queso
  fresco

* Nopales can be found at specialty greengrocers,
farmers' markets and tinned at Latin food stores.

Using gardening gloves, peel the top surface of each nopal with a very sharp
knife to remove the thorns. Wash well under cold water.

Cut each nopal into 1 cm (½ in) strips.

Place the nopales, 500 ml (17 fl oz/2 cups) water and the salt in a saucepan over
a high heat and bring to the boil. Once boiled, drain the water – this will remove
the slimy liquid that is released from the nopales. Cover again with fresh water
and return to the heat, bringing to the boil once again. Reduce the heat to low
and simmer for 15 minutes or until the nopales are very tender.

Meanwhile, to make the dressing, mix the remaining ingredients, except the
cheese, in a bowl and stir until well combined.

Drain the nopales and rinse well. Place the nopales on a serving plate and pour
the dressing over the top. Serve with the queso fresco scattered over the top.

Serves 8 as a side dish

ARROZ A LA MEXICANA
· Mexican rice ·

According to my mum, the secret to this perfect
Mexican rice is the celery.

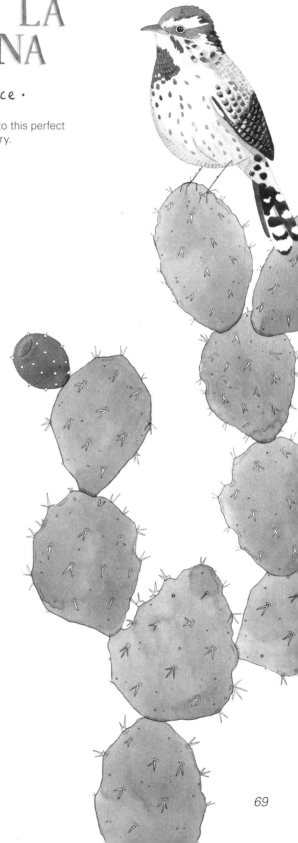

80 ml (2½ fl oz/⅓ cup) olive oil
2 large garlic cloves, crushed
1 fresh jalapeño
370 g (13 oz) long-grain white rice
250 ml (8½ fl oz/1 cup) salt-free tomato juice (do not
  use passata/puréed tomatoes)
½ small white onion, quartered
1 litre (34 fl oz/4 cups) chicken stock
5 coriander (cilantro) stalks
1 celery stalk with young leaves
155 g (5½ oz) fresh, tinned or frozen peas

Heat the olive oil in a large frying pan
over a medium heat. Add the garlic and
jalapeño and sauté for a minute or two
until the jalapeño has changed colour.
Be careful not to burn the garlic. Add
the rice and stir for a few minutes,
ensuring that every grain of rice is
coated with oil.

Place the tomato juice and onion in a
blender and process until smooth.

When the rice has become opaque,
add the tomato and onion mixture and
stir through the rice. Add the remaining
ingredients.

Reduce the heat to medium–low.
Cover the pan but leave a small
opening for the steam to escape and
cook for 15–20 minutes or until
the rice is tender.

Serves 6 as a side dish

BARBACOA

• slow-cooked barbecue •

This is one of the most traditional Mexican dishes and is famous at the
Arroyo restaurant in Mexico City. Traditionally, mutton is wrapped in maguey leaves
(the outer membrane of the agave plant) and slow-cooked in coals underground for at
least 8 hours. The following recipe does not use maguey leaves, and you don't need to
cook it in an underground pit! But the flavours are of true Mexican barbacoa.
It makes a great dinner party dish.

1 leg of mutton or lamb, approximately
  3–4 kg (6 lb 10 oz–8 lb 13 oz)
1 litre (34 fl oz/4 cups) water
2 teaspoons rock salt
1 teaspoon mixed peppercorns
4 onions, quartered
2 garlic bulbs, unpeeled

6 bay leaves
4 carrots, cut into 2 cm (¾ in) pieces
4 tablespoons dried oregano
4 tablespoons dried marjoram
60 ml (2 fl oz/¼ cup) white vinegar
tortillas (see page 72) to serve

Preheat the oven to 160°C (320°F).

Place all the ingredients, except the tortillas, in a large casserole dish. Cover with a lid
or cover tightly with foil and bake in the oven for 6–8 hours or until the meat is falling
off the bone and the liquid has almost evaporated. Check every hour to ensure the
meat is not drying out. Add a little water if it becomes too dry.

When ready to serve, flake the tender meat away from the bone and arrange
on a serving platter. Serve immediately.

Serve the barbacoa with the tortillas, Chicharrón (page 71), Ensalada de nopales
(page 68), Arroz a la Mexicana (page 69) and a variety of salsas.

Serves 6

unwrapping ↗
the barbacoa

off to the kitchen
ready to eat!

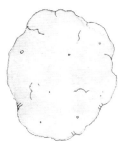

CHICHARRÓN

·salted pork crackling·

500 g (1 lb 2 oz) pork skin, fat removed, cut into bite-sized pieces
sea salt
500 ml (17 fl oz/2 cups) vegetable oil (not olive oil) for frying

Bring 2 litres (68 fl oz/8 cups) water to the boil in a large saucepan or stockpot over a high heat and add the pork. Reduce the heat to low and allow to simmer for about 30 minutes or until cooked.

Remove the pork skin from the pan and pat dry with paper towels. Sprinkle with sea salt.

Preheat the oven to 160°C (320°F).

Place the skin on a greased baking tray (make sure the pieces don't touch, to prevent sticking). Bake in the oven for 50–60 minutes or until very dry.

Heat the vegetable oil in a deep saucepan over a high heat and, when almost smoking (be very careful!), add the pork skin pieces, a few at a time, and cook for 2–3 minutes or until brown and crisp. Remove from the oil with a slotted spoon and drain on paper towels.

Arrange the pork on a platter, sprinkle with salt and serve alongside slow-cooked barbecued meat (see opposite). These are also perfect as a snack with a cold beer.

Makes 200 g (7 oz)

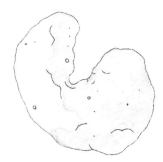

TORTILLAS DE COMAL

·fresh corn tortillas·

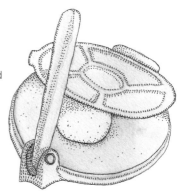

The first part of this recipe makes masa dough, which is used in many delicious recipes, not just for making tortillas!

240 g (8½ oz/2 cups) masa harina flour
250 ml (8½ fl oz/1 cup) hot water
2 tablespoons olive oil

Place the flour in a bowl with the water and olive oil. Mix together to form a dough and then let rest for 20 minutes before using.

When ready, roll the dough into walnut-sized balls. Using a tortilla press, flatten the dough balls to form your tortillas. (It is easier to peel your tortillas from the tortilla press by lining each side of the press with baking paper.)

If you don't have a tortilla press, sandwich the masa dough balls between 2 pieces of baking paper and roll out with a rolling pin to 2 mm (1/16 in) thick and 15 cm (6 in) in diameter.

To cook, place a lightly oiled frying pan over a high heat. Place the tortillas in the pan, one at a time, cooking them for about 2 minutes on each side or until the edges begin to colour. Wrap your cooked tortillas in a clean tea towel (dish towel) to keep warm.

Makes 12 large tortillas

tortilla making is
mesmerising to watch

CALDO XOCHITL
· hot flower soup ·

For the soup:

2 free-range, boneless, skinless chicken
   breasts
4 litres (135 fl oz/16 cups) water
1 large white onion, quartered
2 red chillies, seeded and membranes
   removed, sliced
5 black peppercorns
¼ bunch of coriander (cilantro),
   roughly chopped
4–5 sprigs each of fresh oregano, marjoram,
   thyme and flat-leaf (Italian) parsley
1 bay leaf

2 large carrots, chopped
1 teaspoon white vinegar
½ teaspoon salt

For the corn tortilla 'totopos':

2 stale corn tortillas
vegetable oil for frying

For the garnish:

2 avocados, cubed
fresh coriander (cilantro) leaves
6 lime wedges
salsa of your choice

Place all the soup ingredients in a large saucepan or stockpot over a high heat and bring to the boil. Reduce the heat to low and simmer until the chicken breasts are very tender, about 25 minutes.

To make the totopos, cut the tortillas into wedges. Heat the vegetable oil over a medium–high heat in a frying pan and fry the tortilla wedges until crisp and golden. Drain on paper towels and set aside.

Remove the chicken from the stock and shred the meat. Divide the chicken equally between 8 serving bowls and add a ladleful of the stock and some of the carrot to each bowl. Top with the avocado, coriander leaves and totopos. Serve immediately with lime wedges and the salsa of your choice.

Serves 8

CABRITO EN CERVEZA

· goat in beer jus ·

2.5 kg (5½ lb) leg of goat, cut into
   pieces (ask your butcher to do this)
10 fresh oregano sprigs
6 oven bags for cooking*

* The oven bags will keep the goat nice and moist and
stop the meat from drying out.

For the beer jus:

1 kg (2 lb 3 oz) goat's bones
125 ml (4 fl oz/½ cup) extra-virgin
   olive oil
350 ml (12 fl oz) stout (dark beer)
1 litre (34 fl oz/4 cups) beef stock

Preheat the oven to 160°C (320°F).

Divide the goat pieces and oregano equally between the 6 oven bags. Season with
salt and pepper. Place the bags on a baking tray and set aside.

On a separate baking tray place the goat bones and dress with the olive oil.

Place both the goat bones (leave uncovered) and the tray with the bagged goat meat
in the oven. Bake for 3–4 hours or until the meat is very tender.

Slowly open the cooking bags. The bags will release steam, so be careful you don't
burn yourself. Pour any cooking juices from the goat meat into a bowl and set aside
for the jus. At this point place the goat in the refrigerator. It will be reheated when
ready to serve.

To make the jus, take the goat bones out of the oven and place them in a deep
saucepan. Add the stout and bring to the boil over a high heat. Reduce the heat to
low and simmer for 10 minutes. Add the goat juices and beef stock and continue
to simmer for 40 minutes, stirring occasionally, until the liquid has reduced to the
consistency of gravy. Remove the bones. Strain the liquid through a fine sieve.

Turn the oven up to 180°C (350°F). When ready to serve, place the goat meat onto
a baking tray and cover with foil. Return to the oven for 15 minutes or until hot.

To serve, debone the goat meat and arrange it on a serving platter. Pour the hot jus
over the meat and serve immediately.

This dish goes well with fresh tortillas (see page 72) and Ensalada de nopales (page 68).

Serves 6

PAVO EN MOLE NEGRO

· turkey in black mole sauce ·

1 small turkey (2.5 kg/5½ lb), jointed
1 kg (2 lb 3 oz) pork neck bones
3–4 litres (101–135 fl oz/12–16 cups)
   water
4 white onions, quartered
10 garlic cloves
1½ teaspoons salt
50 g (1¾ oz/⅓ cup) peanuts
50 g (1¾ oz/⅓ cup) almonds
50 g (1¾ oz/⅓ cup) sesame seeds
10 dried mulato chillies
8 dried ancho chillies
125 ml (4 fl oz/½ cup) hot water
75 g (2¾ oz) lard
1 stale corn tortilla
10 cm (4 in) piece stale baguette,
   torn into pieces

1 avocado leaf*
750 g (1 lb 11 oz) ripe tomatoes
1 cinnamon stick
1 teaspoon dried oregano
75 g (2¾ oz) 'Ibarra' chocolate**
6 sweet peppercorns
6 cloves

To serve:

toasted sesame seeds
fresh tortillas (see page 72)
steamed white rice

* Available from some greengrocers. 2 fresh basil
leaves may be substituted.

** Ibarra chocolate is available at specialist delicatessens.
You can substitute with 70% bitter dark chocolate, but
Ibarra will give a more traditional taste.

Preheat the oven to 180°C (350°F). Place the turkey pieces and the pork bones in
a large saucepan or stockpot over a high heat. Add enough water to cover, along
with the onions, garlic and ½ teaspoon of the salt. Bring to the boil and then
reduce the heat to low and allow to simmer for about 40 minutes.

Meanwhile, for the mole sauce, toast the peanuts, almonds and sesame seeds
for about 10 minutes in the oven. Be careful not to let the nuts and seeds brown
or your mole will taste burnt.

Place the chillies in a deep frying pan over a high heat and dry-roast them until
they are soft and starting to release their oils. Remove from the heat.

Remove the stems from the chillies along with the seeds and membranes. Soak
in the hot water and the remaining salt for 30 minutes. Drain and pat dry with
paper towels.

In a large casserole dish, melt the lard. Add the chillies and fry one at a time and
remove. Repeat the process with the tortilla, bread and avocado leaf. Cook each
one and set aside.

Once the turkey is cooked, place the chillies, tortilla, bread, roasted nuts and seeds
and avocado leaf in a blender with about 60 ml (2 fl oz/¼ cup) of the turkey stock.
Process until a smooth paste forms. Fry this mixture in the remaining hot lard,
stirring constantly for about 5 minutes. In the same blender, process the tomatoes
until smooth and add to the paste along with the cinnamon, oregano and the
chocolate cut into pieces, and about 750 ml–1 litre (25½–34 fl oz/3–4 cups)
of the turkey stock.

Simmer over a low heat for about 15 minutes. Add the turkey pieces and
continue cooking until the turkey is very tender and the sauce has thickened.
Serve topped with toasted sesame seeds, fresh hot corn tortillas and white rice.

Serves 6

Abuelo with four
of his daughters

Uncle Juan & proud Abuelo
on Juan's first day working
as a doctor

'CHIVO'

'Chivo' the goat was my
mum's beloved pet when
she was a child. He lived
with the family in Abuelo's
big house. Not a typical urban pet!

Abuelo with my cousin Itzel

Abuelo, Uncle Elias
& Abuela

♥ Abuela & Abuelo ♥

later years

'CHU-CHUS'

'Chu-chus' the rabbit was another
of my mum's childhood pets.
She would feed him carrots &
alfalfa sprouts and he loved her.

COMIDA DEL RANCHO

LOS ARRAYANES

RANCH FOOD

As a young boy, Abuelo began his dream of owning a horse-breeding ranch. The first horse he ever bought cost him 20 pesos, a small fortune in those days. The horse was a young grey female he named La Canica ('the marble'). Abuelo trained her and eventually ran her at the local race track in Alvarado. Mum isn't sure if La Canica ever made Abuelo any money but she recalls that she was a much-loved pet-turned-worker, providing Abuelo with a valuable means of transportation.

Many years later, when he was a successful doctor and businessman, Abuelo bought a ranch in Querétaro outside of Mexico City, named Los Arrayanes, where he built stud and breeding stables, eventually breeding over 100 horses. Most of them were taken to Mexico City at two years of age and sold to racehorse aficionados. But some were kept by Abuelo, trained by a loyal team of trainers, and most of them won him many races. Abuelo named a number of his horses after my sister, Carmen, and me. We visited Los Arrayanes every time we went to Mexico.

I also remember, with a rumbling tummy at the thought, the food Abuela, my mum and my aunties prepared at Los Arrayanes. They would drive to the local market and get fresh produce and goods from the butcher and prepare a feast.

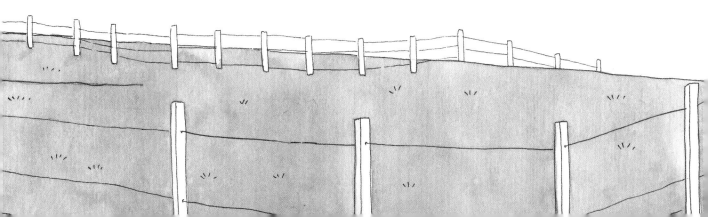

ARROZ CON CHORIZO

• rice with chorizo •

1 x 10 cm (4 in) long chorizo sausage,
  finely chopped
2 tablespoons olive oil
1 fresh jalapeño
½ white onion, finely chopped
2 garlic cloves, crushed (no need to peel)
400 g (14 oz/2 cups) long-grain white rice
750 ml (25½ fl oz/3 cups) chicken stock
½ celery stalk, with some of the leaves
kernels from 1 fresh corn cob
½ red capsicum (bell pepper), cut into thin strips
7 g (¼ oz/¼ cup) coriander (cilantro) leaves,
  chopped

Heat a heavy frying pan over a medium heat and add the chorizo. Allow the natural
oil of the chorizo to be released before adding the olive oil. Add the jalapeño and stir.
After a few minutes, when the jalapeño has changed colour, add the onion and garlic
and continue stirring for a further minute to prevent them from burning.

Add the rice and stir to combine well. Stir every now and then to prevent the rice from
burning. When the rice grains have turned opaque, after a couple of minutes, add the
stock, celery, corn kernels, capsicum and coriander.

Bring to the boil, and then cover the pan. Reduce the heat to low and allow to simmer
for a further 20 minutes or until all the stock has evaporated and the rice is tender.

Serves 4 as a side dish

SALSAS

guajillo

• Salsa volcánica •

100 g (3½ oz) dried cascabel chillies,
    stems removed
100 g (3½ oz) dried guajillo chillies,
    stems removed
50 g (1¾ oz) dried árbol chillies, stems
    removed
1 cinnamon stick
4 cloves
8 pink peppercorns
½ teaspoon ground cumin
1 teaspoon dried oregano
100 ml (3½ fl oz) white vinegar
1 large white onion, quartered

4 garlic cloves
½ teaspoon salt

Place all the ingredients in a blender or
food processor and process until the
mixture is smooth. Add a little water if
necessary to make a smooth paste.

Makes around 500 g (1 lb 2 oz/2 cups).
Store in a glass jar with a lid in the
refrigerator for 2–3 weeks or freeze in
an ice cube tray and use small amounts
as needed. This is a very hot sauce and
only a small amount is required to get a
big kick.

árbol

• Salsa cascabel •

8 green tomatillos, roughly chopped
    (use tinned if you can't find fresh)
4–6 dried cascabel chillies
3 garlic cloves
100 ml (3½ fl oz) white vinegar
½ teaspoon salt

Place the tomatillos and 250 ml
(8½ fl oz/1 cup) water in a saucepan
over a high heat. Bring to the boil,
reduce the heat to low and simmer
for about 5 minutes.

In a frying pan over a high heat, dry-fry
the chillies until they become soft and
release their oils. Remove the stems
(retain the seeds).

Place the tomatillo, chillies, garlic,
vinegar and salt in a blender or food
processor and process until smooth.

Makes around 500 g (1 lb 2 oz/2 cups).
Store in a glass jar with a lid in the
refrigerator for 2–3 weeks. This is a hot
sauce, so you don't need much!

cascabel

• Salsa azteca •

4 large ripe tomatoes, peeled,
    quartered and seeded
1 small red capsicum (bell pepper),
    seeded and membrane removed,
    roughly sliced
3 jalapeños, stems removed
1 large white onion, quartered
2 teaspoons sugar
100 ml (3½ fl oz) white vinegar
2 teaspoons salt
1 teaspoon ground cloves
¼ teaspoon ground cinnamon

Place all the ingredients in a blender
or food processor and process until
smooth. Add a little water if necessary.

Makes around 500 g (1 lb 2 oz/2 cups).
Store in a glass jar with a lid in the
refrigerator for 2–3 weeks. This is a
moderately hot sauce.

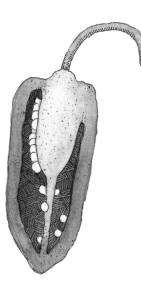

jalapeño

SOPA DE FRIJOLES

· bean soup ·

440 g (15½ oz/2 cups) dried black beans, cooked
2 garlic cloves, finely chopped
500 ml (17 fl oz/2 cups) milk
60 ml (2 fl oz/¼ cup) pouring (single/light) cream
500 ml (17 fl oz/2 cups) chicken stock
20 g (¾ oz) butter
1 slice stale Bolillo (see page 46), made into
   crumbs, or 1 slice white bread, cut into cubes
60 g (2 oz/¼ cup) sour cream
7 g (¼ oz) chopped coriander (cilantro) leaves
   or flat-leaf (Italian) parsley

In a food processor or blender, process the beans, garlic, milk, cream and stock.
This may need to be done in 2 or 3 batches.

Place the mixture in a large saucepan or stockpot over a medium–high heat
and bring gently to the boil. Reduce the heat to low and allow to simmer for
10 minutes. Season with salt and pepper to taste.

In a shallow frying pan, melt the butter. Add the bolillo crumbs or bread pieces
and fry gently for a few minutes or until golden.

Serve this soup very hot topped with the croutons, a tablespoon of sour cream
and the coriander or parsley.

Serves 6

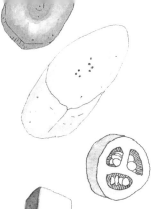

CALDO LOCO

• 'crazy broth' •

For the soup:

2 kg (4 lb 6 oz) hen (or chicken), jointed
2 white onions, quartered
4 garlic cloves, smashed
2 fresh or dried bay leaves
1 celery stalk, roughly chopped
2 cloves
1 teaspoon dried marjoram
7 g (¼ oz) coriander (cilantro) or
   flat-leaf (Italian) parsley leaves
1.5 litres (51 fl oz/6 cups) chicken stock
1 teaspoon white vinegar
2 cloves

For the vegetables:

2 zucchini (courgettes), roughly chopped
2 carrots, roughly chopped
3 potatoes, quartered
2 large plantains, cut into 4 pieces
3 corn cobs, sliced into thirds
80 g (2¾ oz/½ cup) pineapple pieces
1 green apple, cut into small dice

For the chilli seasoning:

60 g (2 oz) lard or 60 ml (2 fl oz/¼ cup)
   olive oil
1 white onion, thinly sliced
2 garlic cloves, crushed
1 clove
3 black peppercorns
2 long red chillies, seeded and
   membranes removed
4 jalapeños, seeded and membranes
   removed, sliced
1 teaspoon ground cumin
¼ teaspoon ground cinnamon
1 fresh bay leaf
125 ml (4 fl oz/½ cup) water
½ teaspoon salt

To serve:
½ lime
crusty bread

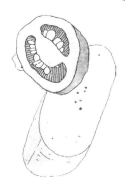

Place all the soup ingredients in a large saucepan or stockpot over a high heat and bring to the boil. Reduce the heat to low and allow to simmer until the chicken is just tender, about 1 hour.

Remove the chicken from the stock. Strain the stock, using a fine sieve, into a clean saucepan or stockpot. Return the chicken to the pan and set aside.

To prepare the chilli seasoning, heat the lard in a shallow frying pan over a medium heat. Add the onion and cook for a few minutes until translucent. Add the remaining ingredients, except the water and the salt. Cook for a further 5 minutes. Transfer the mixture to a blender with the water and salt and process until smooth.

Add the chilli mixture to the chicken stock along with the vegetables and bring to the boil over a high heat. Reduce the heat to low and allow to simmer for about 15 minutes or until the potatoes are tender.

Serve the broth with a squeeze of lime juice and crusty bread.

Serves 6

POZOLE

. ancient Mesoamerican soup .

Pozole, literally meaning 'foamy', is a very special soup dating back to ancient Mesoamerica where it had ritual significance for the Aztecs. With the main ingredient of hominy, a type of dried corn, pozole was considered a sacred dish.

For the soup:

1.8 kg (4 lb) chicken, in portions/jointed
1 kg (2 lb 3 oz) pork (leg is best), cut
  into 5 cm (2 in) cubes
1 large onion
500 g (1 lb 2 oz) hominy*
½ garlic bulb, cloves separated
3 dried ancho chillies
2 dried cascabel or guajillo chillies
½ teaspoon salt
1 teaspoon cumin seeds, pan-roasted
  then ground
1 teaspoon dried oregano

For the garnish:

shredded lettuce (iceberg works best)
thinly sliced radishes
finely chopped green chillies
finely chopped red and white onion
hot tortillas (see page 72)

* Hominy is corn that has been through a special soaking process. You can find it in tins at specialist delicatessens.

Place all the soup ingredients in a large saucepan or stockpot, except the cumin and oregano, adding enough water to cover. Bring to the boil over a high heat, then reduce the heat to low and allow to simmer for about 1 hour or until the chicken and pork are tender and falling off the bone.

Remove the chicken and pork from the stock, then remove the meat from the bones and set aside. Remove the onion, garlic cloves and chillies from the stock and set aside. The only ingredient left in the stock should be the hominy.

Place the cooked onion and garlic, the cumin, oregano and 125 ml (4 fl oz/½ cup) of the stock in a blender and process until smooth. Strain through a fine sieve back into the pan.

Now place the cooked chillies in the blender with a further 125 ml (4 fl oz/½ cup) of the stock and process until smooth. Strain through a fine sieve back into the saucepan, as you did with the onion and garlic mixture.

Return the chicken and pork meat to the pan and season to taste. Return to the heat and simmer gently over a low heat for another 10 minutes.

To serve, place a ladle of broth and a good portion of the meat in each bowl and top with the garnish. Eat with fresh, hot corn tortillas. ¡Exquisito!

Serves 8

CODORNICES RELLENAS

·stuffed quail with sherry·

From time to time Abuelo enjoyed recipes from his Spanish ancestors like this one, which Abuela would often make for him. These quail are great served with white rice, crusty French bread or buttered potatoes.

6 quail
100 g (3½ oz) minced (ground) beef
100 g (3½ oz) minced (ground) pork
1 egg, beaten
1 white onion, finely chopped
2 garlic cloves, crushed
½ jalapeño, seeded and membrane
  removed, thinly sliced
1 teaspoon dried marjoram
1 tablespoon chopped flat-leaf (Italian)
  parsley

¼ teaspoon ground cinnamon
½ teaspoon salt
6 large pitted prunes
100 g (3½ oz) pork pâté
50 g (1¾ oz) butter
60 ml (2 fl oz/¼ cup) dry sherry
125 ml (4 fl oz/½ cup) chicken stock

Clean the quail well and rub them with salt and pepper inside and out.

In a bowl mix the minced meat, egg, onion, garlic, chilli, herbs, cinnamon, the salt and pepper to taste.

Stuff the quail by placing a prune inside each bird's cavity, followed by one-sixth of the pâté (about a tablespoon) and 2 tablespoons of the mince mixture. Seal the birds' cavities with a couple of toothpicks.

In a large frying pan over a medium heat, melt the butter until it foams. Brown the quail in the butter until golden, 3–5 minutes. Add the sherry and stock and cover the pan. Reduce the heat to low and simmer the quail for 20–25 minutes or until tender and the stuffing is cooked. Serve immediately.

Serves 6

ENCHILADAS DE PATO

· duck enchiladas ·

These are a delicious variation on the traditional chicken enchiladas.

For the duck:

2.5 kg (5½ lb) duck, jointed
1 large white onion, quartered
3 garlic cloves
½ green apple, quartered
½ teaspoon salt
60 ml (2 fl oz/¼ cup) olive oil for frying

To serve:

750 ml (25½ fl oz/3 cups) mole negro
  (see page 75)
12 corn tortillas (see page 72)
grated queso fresco
¼ white onion, thinly sliced
iceberg lettuce
3–4 radishes, thinly sliced

Place all the ingredients for the duck, except the olive oil, in a large saucepan or stockpot over a high heat and bring to the boil. Reduce the heat to low and simmer for 45 minutes or until the duck is tender. Remove from the heat. Let the duck cool in the stock then drain.

Remove the duck meat from the bones.

In a large frying pan over a high heat, fry the duck meat in the oil for a few minutes, until just golden brown but not dry.

Assemble the enchiladas by heating the mole negro in a saucepan over a medium heat for around 5 minutes or until hot. Meanwhile, dip the tortillas in hot water briefly then wrap them in a clean tea towel (dish towel) and place in the microwave for 15–20 seconds on high (100%). Keep the tortillas wrapped in the tea towel until they are needed.

When the mole begins to boil, dip 1 tortilla at a time in the hot sauce and place on a serving platter. Place 2 tablespoons of duck meat on each tortilla and fold the tortilla over. Continue this process until all the tortillas are used.

Pour any remaining mole sauce over the enchiladas and top with the queso fresco. At this stage the enchiladas can be kept in a low oven to keep warm before serving.

To serve, top the enchiladas with the white onion and garnish with the lettuce and radish slices on the side. Serve immediately with Arroz a la Mexicana (page 69) and refried beans, if desired.

Serves 4

BIRRIA

·neck of beef in spicy broth·

2 kg (4 lb 6 oz) beef neck (on the bone)
3 guajillo chillies
2 ancho chillies
5 garlic cloves, finely chopped
2 white onions, finely chopped
4 bay leaves
1 teaspoon dried thyme
1 teaspoon dried oregano
3 cloves
4–5 litres (135–169 fl oz/16–20 cups)
    water (enough to cover the meat)

2 tablespoons white vinegar
1 teaspoon salt
1 teaspoon pepper
Salsa para birria (see opposite)

To serve:

tortillas (see page 72)
finely chopped white onion
chopped coriander (cilantro) leaves

Place all the ingredients, except the salsa, in a large saucepan or stockpot. Bring to the boil over a high heat. Reduce the heat to low and simmer for 3–4 hours until the beef is very tender and flakes away from the bone. Remove the beef pieces from the pan and discard the bones. Set the meat aside and keep warm.

Return the broth to the heat and add the salsa para birria to taste and simmer for 5 minutes.

Divide the meat into 6 portions and place in bowls. Add a ladle of the broth to each.

To serve, place bits of beef on the tortillas to make soft tacos, and top with the finely chopped white onion and coriander. You can add extra salsa if you like it hot. Enjoy the broth between bites of the taco.

Serves 8

SALSA PARA BIRRIA

· chilli sauce for Birria ·

500 g (1 lb 2 oz) ripe tomatoes,
    quartered
500 g (1 lb 2 oz) tomatillos, quartered
½ white onion, finely chopped
5 small red chillies or 3 habanero
    chillies, seeded and membranes
    removed if you prefer your salsa mild

2 garlic cloves, finely chopped
1 teaspoon lime juice
1 fresh bay leaf
1 teaspoon dried oregano

Place the tomatoes, tomatillos, onion and chillies in a small saucepan with 125 ml (4 fl oz/½ cup) water over a high heat. Bring to the boil. Remove from the heat.

Remove the skin from the tomatoes and place in a blender with the remaining ingredients. Blend until smooth. Season to taste and the sauce is ready to use.

Makes 750 ml (25½ fl oz/3 cups)

my dad, mum, Aunty Beatriz,
Abuelo & Abuela at Los Arrayanes

me, riding a horse around
the stables

inspecting the stables

Abuelo adored his horses

little cowboys
(my cousins)

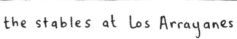

the stables at Los Arrayanes

SALPICÓN

· pulled beef salad ·

800 g (1 lb 12 oz) beef brisket, cut into
   4 pieces
5 pink peppercorns
5 black peppercorns
3 cloves
2 bay leaves, torn in half
1 large white onion, quartered
3 garlic cloves, lightly crushed
1 teaspoon salt
1 tablespoon white vinegar

For the dressing:

125 ml (4 fl oz/½ cup) extra-virgin
   olive oil
juice of 2 limes
2 tablespoons white wine vinegar
1 small red onion, thinly sliced
2 teaspoons dried oregano
1 teaspoon sugar

To serve:

cos (romaine) lettuce leaves
10 g (¼ oz/⅓ cup) coriander (cilantro)
   leaves
½ red onion, thinly sliced into rings
4 hard-boiled eggs, quartered
2 tomatoes, quartered
2 radishes, thinly sliced
tortillas (see page 72) or tostadas

Place all the ingredients for the beef in a deep saucepan over a high heat, adding enough water to cover the meat. Bring to the boil, skimming any residue that comes to the surface.

Reduce the heat to low and simmer for approximately 3 hours or until the beef comes apart easily with a fork. Drain and allow the meat to cool, then pull strands of the meat apart and place them in a bowl. Cover the bowl with plastic wrap and place in the refrigerator until ready to serve.

Place all the ingredients for the dressing in a small jar and shake until well combined.

To assemble the dish, arrange the beef on a serving platter that has been lined with the lettuce leaves. Scatter the coriander and onion rings on top. Arrange the hard-boiled eggs, tomato and radish slices around the meat. Serve with tortillas or tostadas.

Serves 4

LA GRANJA
(the farm)

PATITAS DE PUERCO EN ESCABECHE

·pigs' trotters in brine·

For the pigs' trotters:

6 pigs' trotters, halved
1 large white onion, quartered
½ garlic bulb
1 bay leaf
½ teaspoon dried oregano
1 teaspoon salt

For the brine:

125 ml (4 fl oz/½ cup) extra-virgin
   olive oil
2 white onions, thinly sliced

4 garlic cloves, halved
3 carrots, thinly sliced
4 jalapeños
4 sweet peppercorns
2 bay leaves
1 teaspoon dried oregano
2 teaspoons dried thyme
2 teaspoons dried marjoram
60 ml (2 fl oz/¼ cup) white vinegar

To serve:
corn (tortilla) chips

Place all the ingredients for the pigs' trotters in a large saucepan over a high heat, adding enough water to cover. Bring to the boil and then reduce the heat to low and simmer for around 2 hours or until the trotters are very tender and the liquid has reduced to about 375 ml (12½ fl oz/1½ cups).

Remove the trotters from the pan and allow to cool slightly. Reserve the liquid – it will turn into a jelly as it cools and will be used for the dressing. When the trotters are cool enough to handle, remove the meat from the bone.

To make the brine, heat the olive oil gently in a saucepan over a medium heat. Add the onion and garlic, sautéing for a few minutes until the onion is soft. Add the carrots, jalapeños, peppercorns, herbs and salt to taste and cook for a further 5 minutes. Add the vinegar and the jelly from the trotters and allow to simmer for a further 2–3 minutes. While still hot, pour the brine over the trotters. Refrigerate for at least 1 hour before serving.

To assemble, place the meat on a serving platter with some corn chips to be eaten as a snack.

Serves 6 as a snack

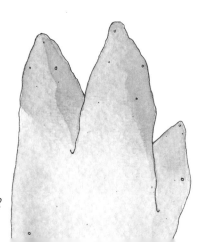
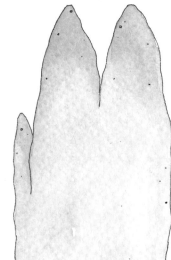
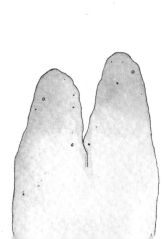

COCIDO ESPAÑOL

· Spanish-style pork belly ·

Another favourite Spanish dish of Abuelo's was this special *cocido* (stew). Abuela learned this recipe from La Gallega (meaning 'the Spaniard'), who was a celebrated Spanish-born chef from Veracruz. Serve with crusty bread or white rice.

1 kg (2 lb 3 oz) pork belly, cut into
  6 pieces
½ teaspoon salt
80 ml (2½ fl oz/⅓ cup) olive oil, plus
  extra for brushing
1 onion, finely chopped
6 garlic cloves, finely chopped
100 g (3½ oz) chorizo, sliced
2 large ripe tomatoes, chopped

2 flat-leaf (Italian) parsley sprigs
1 mint sprig
6 capers
6 green olives, pitted and sliced
3 bay leaves
1 large potato, cubed
1 small green or red chilli, seeded and
  membrane removed

Place the pork belly in a large saucepan with 1 litre (34 fl oz/4 cups) water and the salt over a high heat. Bring to the boil and then reduce the heat to low and simmer for 1 hour, or until the pork belly is tender and the liquid has reduced to about 500 ml (17 fl oz/2 cups). Remove the pork and set the stock aside.

Preheat the oven to 170°C (340°F).

Place the pork, fat side up, on a greased baking tray. Brush the top of the pork with the extra olive oil and bake in the oven for 1 hour or until golden.

In a clean large saucepan, heat the oil over a medium heat and fry the onion and garlic until soft. Add the chorizo and cook for a further 5 minutes. Add the cooked pork and the remaining ingredients, except the potato and chilli, and cook for a further 2–3 minutes.

Add the stock, potato and chilli and bring to the boil, reduce the heat to low and simmer for 10 minutes or until the potato is cooked. Serve hot.

Serves 6

...they cooked marshmallows, played their guitars and drank atole to warm themselves up. They did not go to bed until the fire had gone out. The night sky was an explosion of stars and the soft, scary sound of owls could be heard...

Atole

corn based hot drink.

60 g (2 oz/½ cup) masa harina flour
150 ml (5 fl oz) water
1 litre (34 fl oz/4 cups) full-cream
  (whole) milk
150 g (5½ oz) white sugar
1 cinnamon stick, plus 4 extra sticks
  to serve

In a small bowl, combine the masa harina flour with the water and mix well.

Transfer the masa mix, milk and sugar to a blender or food processor and blend until smooth.

Place the mixture in a saucepan, along with the cinnamon stick, and cook over a low heat until the sugar has dissolved and the mix has slightly thickened, about 5–10 minutes.

Atole is traditionally served in a terracotta mug with a stick of cinnamon to stir the drink with.

Serves 4

Variations: You can add these flavours to the mixture at the blender stage.

Strawberry: 200 g (7 oz) fresh strawberries, washed and hulled
Chocolate: 30 g (1 oz/¼) cup unsweetened (Dutch) cocoa powder
Vanilla: The seeds of 1 vanilla bean
Pecan: 125 g (4½ oz/1¼ cups) pecans, pan-roasted and allowed to cool

GOLOSINAS Y DULCES

CANDY
AND SWEETS

Being a doctor who practised what he preached, Abuelo wasn't a huge
fan of sugary sweets. However, he would always indulge us. Without fail
my sister, cousins and I would be tantalised by the colours and smells of
the sweet (candy) stalls found on most street corners. Even when people
were waiting in traffic, sweet vendors would peddle their goodies to the
idling cars. Abuelo always saw purchasing these sweets as an important
way to support the poor families living nearby.

Some vendors carried enormous baskets with an array of baked goods;
others had long poles on which sugar-coated apples were displayed. Other
vendors carried platters with nut-covered fudges, coconut rounds, various
nut brittles and many more delights.

HUEVOS REALES
·'royal eggs'·

10 egg yolks
40 g (1 ½ oz) butter, softened
2 teaspoons baking powder
1 teaspoon ground cinnamon
40 g (1 ½ oz/⅓ cup) dried muscatel
   grapes or sultanas (golden raisins)

For the syrup:
250 ml (8½ fl oz/1 cup) water
460 g (1 lb/2 cups) caster (superfine)
   sugar
2 cinnamon sticks
60 ml (2 fl oz/¼ cup) dry sherry

Preheat the oven to 170°C (340°F) and grease a 20 cm (8 in) square baking tin.

Beat the egg yolks and butter together using an electric beater until pale. Fold in the baking powder, cinnamon and dried fruit.

Pour the mixture into the baking tin, cover with foil and bake for 40 minutes or until a toothpick inserted in the middle comes out clean.

Meanwhile, for the syrup, place the water with the sugar and cinnamon in a small saucepan over a medium–high heat. Bring to the boil, then reduce the heat to low and simmer, stirring constantly, until the mixture reduces by half and has thickened. This will take around 10–15 minutes. Remove from the heat and stir in the sherry, being carefully as it might spit at you.

When the egg mixture is cooked, remove it from the oven and, using a toothpick, make little holes all over it while it is still in the baking tin; this allows the syrup to be absorbed better. Pour the hot syrup over the egg bake and place in the refrigerator for 1 hour or until set.

When ready to serve, remove the egg bake from the baking tin and cut into 5 cm (2 in) squares. Serve with any syrup left over in the pan.

Makes 12 squares

step one:

step two:

step three:

CHONGOS
ZAMORANOS

· curd squares in cinnamon syrup ·

This recipe requires patience and time,
but it is well worth the effort.

1 litre (34 fl oz/4 cups) milk
220 g (8 oz/1 cup) sugar
½ rennet (junket) tablet
1 cinnamon stick

Place the milk and sugar in a medium
saucepan over a medium heat. Stir
constantly until the sugar has dissolved.

Turn off the heat.

Dissolve the rennet tablet in a little
water and add it to the milk mixture.
Leave the milk mixture in the saucepan
for 2–3 hours in the refrigerator to set.

Once set (and still in the saucepan)
cut into 5 cm (2 in) squares (roughly as
some pieces will have the round edge
of the pan). Break the cinnamon into
pieces and insert a piece of cinnamon
stick into each square.

Return the saucepan to a very low
heat. Do not allow to boil. Keep on the
stove for around 2–3 hours without
disturbing until the squares have turned
a light golden brown and the liquid has
reduced and turned syrupy.

Allow to cool before serving.

Makes 16 pieces

step four:

step five:

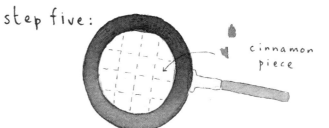

cinnamon
piece

aerial view

DULCE DE COCO

· coconut puddings ·

grated flesh of 1 fresh coconut or
  300 g (10½ oz/5 cups) store-bought
  soft shredded coconut
250 ml (8½ fl oz/1 cup) coconut water
220 g (8 oz/1 cup) sugar
3 egg yolks
60 ml (2 fl oz/¼ cup) dry sherry

Carefully halve the coconut using a hammer or heavy butcher's knife.

With a very sharp knife, loosen the white flesh from the coconut shell. It will come away easily. Grate the coconut into a deep saucepan. Add the coconut water and sugar. Bring to the boil over a high heat and then simmer until the coconut becomes translucent and the syrup has thickened slightly, about 15 minutes.

Remove from the heat and allow to cool a little.

Meanwhile, beat the egg yolks with the sherry in a bowl for about 2 minutes. Add the egg mixture to the pan with the coconut and return to the stove over a low heat. Stirring often to prevent it from burning, cook until the mixture has thickened. This should take around 15 minutes. Remove from the stove and allow to cool completely.

To serve, pour into four individual ramekins and, using a kitchen blowtorch, torch the mixture until the surface is golden and caramelised. Serve immediately.

Makes 4

DULCE DE GUAYABA

·guava paste·

250 g (9 oz) guavas, peeled
185 ml (6 fl oz) water
juice of ½ lime
250 g (9 oz) white sugar
½ egg white
queso fresco to serve

Place the guavas in a blender or food processor with 60 ml (2 fl oz/¼ cup) of the water and the lime juice. Purée until smooth. Using a fine sieve or a piece of muslin (cheesecloth), strain the guava pulp, discarding the liquid, and place the pulp in a bowl. Set aside.

Place the sugar and remaining water in a small saucepan over a medium heat. With a wooden spoon, stir until the sugar has dissolved and the syrup has reached the soft ball stage (112°C/234°F) on a candy thermometer.

Add the guava pulp and continue cooking over a medium–high heat until the mixture thickens and the base of the pan can be seen when stirring, around 15–20 minutes.

Pour the guava mixture into a bowl and allow to cool. When cool enough to handle, add the egg white and mix with clean hands until the mixture changes colour.

Pour onto a baking tray lined with baking paper and allow to set for a few hours. Serve slices of the paste with queso fresco.

Makes 500 g (1 lb 2 oz)

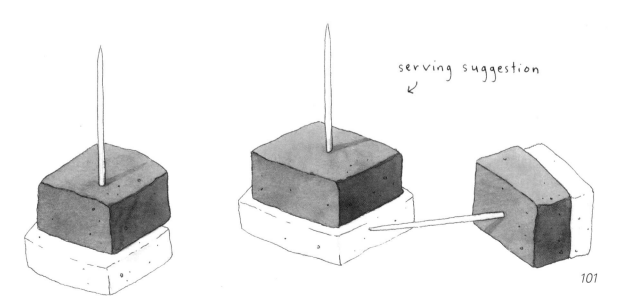

serving suggestion

PALANQUETA BLANCA

· white almond brittle ·

This recipe is a Mexican version of the Spanish *turrón de Alicante*,
a favourite sweet at Christmas time and a favourite of mine.

rice paper for confectionery*
620 g (1 lb 6 oz/4 cups) blanched almonds
440 g (15½ oz/2 cups) sugar
190 ml (6½ fl oz/¾ cup) water
2 teaspoons white vinegar
vegetable oil

* Not to be confused with rice paper for Vietnamese rolls!

Preheat the oven to 180°C (350°F) and line a 25 cm (10 in) square baking tin with
baking paper, allowing the ends to hang over the tin.

Place one layer of rice paper on the bottom of the baking tin, covering the tin's
surface. Set aside.

Place the almonds on a baking tray and roast in the oven for 5–10 minutes or until
slightly golden. Do not brown them or the result will be bitter.

Allow the almonds to cool completely.

Meanwhile, place the sugar, water and vinegar in a heavy saucepan and bring to the
boil over a high heat, stirring continuously. When the syrup reaches the soft ball stage
(112°C/234°F) on a candy thermometer, add the roasted almonds and beat the mixture
vigorously until it turns white. This may take a while but hang in there, as it will be
worth it!

Once the mixture is white, spread it quickly onto the baking tin lined with rice paper.
While still hot, top the palanqueta with another sheet of rice paper, covering the
whole surface. Using a sharp knife, cut the mixture into 16 squares while it is still soft,
separating each piece so the squares don't stick together when set.

Store the squares in an airtight container or wrap in cellophane. These will keep for
around 1–2 weeks.

Makes 16 squares

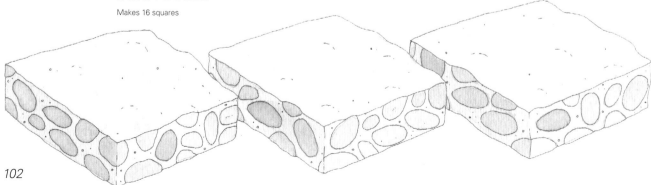

my sister Carmen
attacking a piñata

CACAHUATES GARAPIÑADOS

· sugar coated peanuts ·

A perfect addition to a piñata!

160 g (5½ oz/1 cup) raw peanuts,
  skin left on
220 g (8 oz/1 cup) sugar
125 ml (4 fl oz/½ cup) water
½ teaspoon natural vanilla extract
1–2 drops of red food colouring

Place all the ingredients in a deep frying pan and bring to the boil over a medium–high heat, stirring constantly with a wooden spoon.

Reduce the heat to low and allow to simmer for about 10–15 minutes while continuing to stir. The mixture surrounding the peanuts will become foamy at first and then dry, resembling sand.

Keep stirring constantly until the sugar melts again and coats each peanut. This should take an extra 5 minutes.

Remove from the heat and pour the peanuts on a tray lined with baking paper. Allow the peanuts to cool completely before storing them in an airtight container or cellophane bags. These will keep for 1 week.

Makes 350 g (12½ oz)

me, trying my best!

ROLLO DE NUEZ

· nut log ·

500 ml (17 fl oz/2 cups) milk
250 g (9 oz) sugar
1 vanilla bean, split lengthways and seeds
 scraped
125 ml (4 fl oz/½ cup) pouring (single/
 light) cream
40 g (1½ oz) butter
150 ml (5 fl oz) glucose syrup
⅛ teaspoon bicarbonate of soda
 (baking soda)
150 g (5½ oz/1½ cups) pecans, finely
 chopped, plus 75 g (2¾ oz/¾ cup)
 whole pecans

Place the milk, sugar, vanilla bean and seeds, cream, butter and 2 tablespoons of the glucose syrup in a heavy saucepan over a medium–high heat. Bring to the boil, stirring constantly to prevent the milk from boiling over. After about 10 minutes, when the milk is slightly thicker, add the bicarbonate of soda.

Keep stirring for around 15 minutes more, until the mixture becomes quite thick and the base of the pan can be seen when stirring with a spoon. Remove the vanilla bean and discard.

Add the chopped pecans and continue stirring until well combined. Remove from the heat and keep stirring until the mixture has cooled enough to handle.

Form a log with the fudge. Brush the roll with the remaining glucose syrup (you may need to warm it slightly in the microwave) and cover the surface with the whole pecans.

Wrap in cellophane or store in an airtight container for 2 weeks.

Makes approximately 300 g (10½ oz)

MORELIANAS

· goat's caramel tuiles ·

500 ml (17 fl oz/2 cups) goat's milk
150 g (5½ oz) brown sugar
½ teaspoon natural vanilla extract
⅛ teaspoon bicarbonate of soda
(baking soda)

Preheat the oven to 180°C (350°F).

Place all the ingredients in a heavy saucepan and bring to the boil over a high heat. Stir the mixture continuously for around 5 minutes until the sugar has dissolved. When the mixture reaches boiling point, reduce the heat to low and keep simmering for about 1½ hours, or until the mixture has thickened (the base of the pan should be visible when stirring with a spoon) and is a dark golden brown colour.

The mixture will thicken further as it cools. You have now made cajeta (goat's milk caramel). You can place this in a glass jar and use it as an ice-cream topping, a spread for bread, or just eat it by the spoonful like I do. But, to make morelianas, spread tablespoons of the cajeta very thinly onto a baking tray lined with baking paper. Bake in the oven for 15–25 minutes until the cajeta starts to bubble and dries a little. You'll have to keep your eye on it so it doesn't burn.

Take the morelianas out of the oven and allow to cool for a minute or two. While still soft, peel the morelianas from the baking paper, being careful not to tear them. Allow to cool on a wire rack. Serve as a snack or as a garnish for ice cream.

Makes 20 tuiles

ROMPEDIENTES

·'teeth breakers'·

250 ml (8½ fl oz/1 cup) water
460 g (1 lb/2 cups) caster (superfine) sugar
60 g (2 oz) butter
½ teaspoon natural vanilla extract
80 g (2¾ oz/½ cup) raw unsalted peanuts,
  skinned

Place the water and the sugar in a medium saucepan over a medium heat. Mix with a wooden spoon until the sugar has dissolved. Add the butter and vanilla extract. Reduce the heat to low and allow to simmer for around 10 minutes. Do not stir the mixture at this stage.

When the syrup has reduced by about half and a few drops of it crystallise when dropped into a glass of water, remove it from the heat. Toss in the peanuts and pour onto a greased tray. Allow to cool so you can handle it – but be very careful as the mixture will still be hot and can burn (silicone oven gloves are recommended at this stage).

Shape the toffee mixture into a log. Pull from each end until stretched to twice its length. Fold in half and stretch again to twice its length, fold again, twist and continue with this process until the toffee turns white and has almost become solid. Be careful and work fast – it will still be hot.

Once the toffee is almost solid but still soft, shape it into a log around 3 cm (1¼ in) thick and cut into 3 cm (1¼ in) pieces with a sharp knife or scissors. Set on a plate to cool completely.

These will keep for 3 weeks in an airtight container.

Makes around 30

ALFAJORES DE LECHE

· lime milk fudge ·

These were my Abuelo's favourite treat! As a doctor he usually avoided desserts, but he never turned down these when Abuela made them. The best alfajores were made with fresh milk just taken from the cows. In those days Alvarado was dotted with dairy farms and it was easy to get beautiful, fresh, creamy milk.

500 ml (17 fl oz/2 cups) milk
250 g (9 oz) sugar
zest of 1 lime, kept in 1 cm (½ in) wide strips
extra lime zest, cut into thin strips for garnish

Place the milk, sugar and wide lime zest strips in a large saucepan over a medium heat. Bring to the boil gently, stirring constantly. Reduce the heat to low and allow to simmer for about an hour, stirring often to prevent it from burning. Stick with it, as it will be worth the commitment.

When the milk is reduced to a quarter of its original volume and has thickened (it should resemble the consistency of honey, with a sand-like texture at the base of the pan), remove the pan from the heat and keep stirring until the mixture cools slightly.

Remove the lime zest. Pour the mixture onto a baking tray lined with baking paper and allow to cool.

Cut the fudge into diamonds and arrange on a plate. Top with the curled extra lime zest strips for decoration. Allow to rest until slightly dry.

These will keep for a week in an airtight container – if you can resist eating them all before then!

Makes around 30

ALEGRÍAS

• 'Little joys' •

225 g (8 oz/5 cups) puffed amaranth
70 g (2½ oz/½ cup) pepitas (pumpkin seeds)
100 g (3½ oz/1 cup) pecans, chopped
500 g (1 lb 2 oz) piloncillo* or palm sugar
  (jaggery)
125 ml (4 fl oz/½ cup) honey
1 tablespoon lemon juice or white vinegar

*Piloncillo is a type of hard-packed brown sugar traditionally used
in Mexico. Look for it in Latin food stores.

Dry-fry the amaranth in a large frying pan over a medium heat, stirring constantly for 5 minutes or until golden. Pour onto a large tray and allow to cool completely.

In the same frying pan, toast the pepitas, stirring constantly, for 5 minutes or until they change colour slightly. Remove from the heat and allow to cool.

Repeat the process with the pecans.

Once the amaranth, seeds and nuts are toasted and cooled, mix them together in a bowl.

Break the sugar into small pieces and place it in a large saucepan along with the honey and lemon juice. Bring to the boil gently over a medium heat, stirring constantly.

Reduce the heat to low and simmer for about 15 minutes or until the sugar has dissolved, then remove from the heat. Add the amaranth, seed and nut mixture to the sugar and mix with a wooden spoon until all the ingredients are combined.

Pour the mixture into a 30 x 20 cm (12 x 8 in) shallow baking tin lined with baking paper (make sure the baking paper overhangs at both ends). Using a spatula, press the mixture into the tin to ensure it is compact.

While still warm, cut the mixture into squares with a sharp knife. Allow to cool completely in the tin. To remove from the tin, hold both ends of the baking paper and lift out. Separate the squares and wrap each one individually in cellophane or place in an airtight container.

These will keep for 1 week in an airtight container.

Makes 18 squares

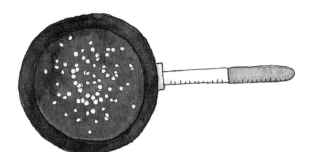

step one:
toast amaranth,
then repeat with
pepitas & pecans

step two:
mix pepitas, pecans
& amaranth in a bowl

step three:
add piloncillo, honey
& lemon to a pan

step four:
add amaranth, seed &
nut mix to the pan
& combine

step five:
pour into a lined
baking tin. Cut
into squares &
allow to set

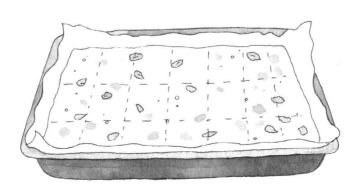

PANADERÍA

SWEET BREADS

One of Abuelo's favourite discoveries in the big capital was the *panaderías* (bakeries). He just loved the *pan dulce* (sweet bread) sold at these establishments to accompany the tall glass of cold milk he would drink for his *merienda* (snack) after attending night school.

There is nothing like walking into a Mexican *panadería* with its delicious smells of buttery, sugary goodies laced with cinnamon, rosewater and vanilla! The range of shapes and textures make you want to eat everything! Abuelo must have been impressed. He soon developed a taste for the delicious French-influenced pastries, which continued to be a favourite until the end of his life.

CONCHAS
• 'sea shells' •

These sweet buns are named after sea shells because of their shape. They have a delicious, crumbly sweet topping that always reminds me of tiger stripes. One of my favourite memories as a child is of sharing conchas with my Abuelo over a mug of Mexican hot chocolate. It wasn't uncommon for this to be dinner – sweet breads are a typical light meal before bed in Mexico. This recipe departs from tradition in that it calls for powdered cake mix, a secret ingredient added by my mum that makes preparation easier and tastes great!

160 g (5½ oz) self-raising flour
340 g (12 oz) buttercake cake mix
1 teaspoon dried yeast dissolved in
  60 ml (2 fl oz/¼ cup) warm water
2 eggs, lightly beaten
½ teaspoon salt
100 g (3½ oz) sugar
65 g (2¼ oz) coconut cream powder
120 g (4½ oz) butter, melted

For the topping:
100 g (3½ oz/⅔ cup) plain (all-purpose)
  flour
100 g (3½ oz) icing (confectioners')
  sugar
pinch of salt
100 g (3½ oz) butter, at room
  temperature
50 ml (1¾ fl oz) water
1 drop of red colouring for pink icing
1 tablespoon unsweetened (Dutch)
  cocoa powder for chocolate icing

Mix the self-raising flour and cake mix in a bowl. Place half the mix on a clean work surface and make a well in the centre. Gently add the remaining ingredients to the mix, except the butter and the rest of the flour/cake mix, and gradually combine with your hands until a sticky dough is formed.

Gradually add the butter and remaining flour/cake mix and combine with your hands until the dough is glossy and elastic. Knead vigorously, bashing the dough on the work surface a few times, for 15 minutes, until bubbles appear under the surface of the dough.

Place the dough in a greased bowl and cover loosely with plastic wrap or a clean damp tea towel (dish towel). Leave in a warm place for 2 hours or until it has doubled in size.

Punch the dough down and knead slightly to form a ball, cover again and leave to rest for a further 2–4 hours. At this point the dough can be placed in the refrigerator and baked the next day if you like.

When the concha dough is ready to use, roll pieces into peach-sized balls with your palms and place them on greased baking trays, leaving room between them.

Flatten each concha lightly. Cover the tray with baking paper and set aside for 1 hour or until doubled in size.

Preheat the oven to 210°C (410°F).

To make the topping, combine the flour, icing sugar and salt in a medium-sized bowl. Using your fingers, mix in the butter and water, alternately, a little bit at a time until the mixture forms a dough that holds its shape. At this stage you can add a teaspoon of red food colouring or cocoa powder (add to just half of the mixture if you'd like to create two different toppings).

Form small apricot-sized balls of the topping mixture. Using a rolling pin, roll out between 2 pieces of baking paper until they resemble small, thin tortillas, around 10 cm (4 in) in diameter.

Peel the topping rounds off the paper and place on top of each concha. Using a sharp knife, cut lines into the topping, avoiding the concha dough (otherwise it will deflate). You can make different designs if you want, but the traditional markings are lines resembling the lines of a sea shell.

Place in the oven for 10 minutes, then reduce the heat to 180°C (350°F) and bake for 5 minutes. These conchas are best enjoyed with a cup of hot chocolate! Conchas store well in a paper bag for 2–3 days. They can also be frozen (for up to 2 months) and thawed at room temperature when ready to eat. Do not attempt to defrost them in the microwave, though, as the topping will melt!

Makes 6–8 large conchas

IGLESIA DE NUESTRA
SEÑORA DEL ROSARIO

MARQUEZOTES DE ALVARADO

· Alvarado sweet bread ·

My Abuelo was addicted to this sweet bread, a Mexican version of Italian biscotti.
It is eaten for breakfast, or as a snack with chocolate, coffee or milk.

9 eggs
220 g (8 oz/1 cup) sugar
225 g (8 oz/1½ cups) plain (all-purpose)
  flour
¼ teaspoon bicarbonate of soda
  (baking soda)
2 tablespoons sesame seeds

Preheat the oven to 160°C (320°F) and grease and line a 25 x 15 cm (10 x 6 in) loaf (bar) tin.

Beat the eggs with the sugar for 5 minutes, or until the eggs are very pale in colour.

In a separate bowl, sift together the flour and bicarbonate of soda. Fold the flour into the beaten eggs very gently.

Pour the mixture into the tin and sprinkle with the sesame seeds. Bake for 20 minutes or until cooked – when a skewer inserted comes out clean.

Remove from the oven and let the bread sit for a further 10 minutes in the tin. Then turn out onto a wire rack to cool.

Once completely cool, cut the cake into 5 cm (2 in) squares, being very careful not to break the bread (it will be quite crumbly).

Line a baking tray with baking paper.

Place the squares on the baking tray and bake for a further 10 minutes or until the bread is very dry and crisp.

These will keep for 1 week in an airtight container.

Makes 12 pieces

OREJAS

• 'ears' •

Orejas are based on French palmiers, small, ear-like, flaky, buttery cookies. My Abuelo's family recipe is a variation on the original, with the addition of ground cinnamon. A tray of sweet breads at *merienda* (snack) time was never complete if orejas were missing.

170 g (6 oz/¾ cup) caster (superfine)
  sugar
4 sheets of frozen puff pastry, thawed
ground cinnamon for dusting

Preheat the oven to 180°C (350°F).

Sprinkle 3 teaspoons of the sugar on one sheet of pastry, dust liberally with cinnamon and press firmly with your fingers to encrust the sugar and cinnamon into the pastry. Cover this sheet with another sheet of pastry and repeat the process with the sugar and cinnamon.

Continue this method until all 4 sheets of pastry are used. You should have a stack of pastry sheets one on top of the other.

Fold about 2 cm (¾ in) of one edge of the pastry onto itself. Repeat this process on the opposite side of the pastry. Continue folding both ends until they meet.

With a very sharp knife, cut crossways slices of pastry around 2 cm (¾ in) thick and arrange them on a baking tray lined with baking paper, leaving enough room for them to expand as they bake.

Dissolve the remaining caster sugar in 60 ml (2 fl oz/¼ cup) water, and then brush over the top of the unbaked orejas. This will give them a lovely crunchy topping.

Bake for 12–15 minutes or until just golden and the sugar is bubbling. Remove from the tray while still hot and allow to cool completely on a wire rack.

These will keep for around 1 week stored in an airtight container.

Makes around 12–15

PANQUÉ DE NARANJA

• colonial orange tea cake •

This cake is a recipe from Spanish colonial times.
Abuelo loved a sliced of this buttery, aromatic sweet cake.

100 g (3½ oz) butter
145 g (5 oz/⅔ cup) caster (superfine)
  sugar
3 eggs
juice and zest of 1 orange
1 teaspoon natural vanilla extract
30 ml (1 fl oz) sweet sherry
150 g (5½ oz/1 cup) plain (all-purpose)
  flour
¼ teaspoon salt
1½ teaspoons baking powder

Preheat the oven to 180°C (350°F) and grease and line a 25 x 15 cm
(10 x 6 in) loaf (bar) tin.

Using an electric mixer, beat the butter and sugar until creamy. Add the
eggs and beat well. Add the orange juice and zest, vanilla and sherry,
mixing well.

Sift the flour, salt and baking powder into the wet ingredients and mix
until combined.

Pour the mixture into the tin and bake for 25–30 minutes or until the top is
golden brown and a skewer inserted comes out clean.

Allow to cool on a wire rack before serving.

This will keep for a few days in an airtight container.

Serves 8

COCHINITOS DE PILONCILLO
· piggy cookies ·

300 g (10½ oz) piloncillo*, or brown
   sugar or grated palm sugar (jaggery)
100 ml (3½ fl oz) boiling water
100 ml (3½ fl oz) vegetable oil (not
   olive oil)
1 teaspoon natural vanilla extract (or
   ouzo liqueur for an aniseed flavour)
1 teaspoon bicarbonate of soda
   (baking soda)

*Piloncillo is a type of hard-packed brown sugar
traditionally used in Mexico. Look for it in Latin
food stores.

10 g (¼ oz) baking powder
550 g (1 lb 3 oz/3⅔ cups) plain (all-
   purpose) flour
1 teaspoon ground cinnamon
icing (confectioners') sugar for dusting
   (optional)

For the glaze:
1 tablespoon water
1 tablespoon caster (superfine) sugar

Preheat the oven to 180°C (350°F) and line 2 baking trays with baking paper.

In a large mixing bowl dissolve the piloncillo in the boiling water. Allow the water to cool down and, when it reaches tepid stage, add the vegetable oil, vanilla, bicarbonate of soda and baking powder. Mix until combined.

Sift the flour and cinnamon together and then gradually add the flour to the sugar mixture, half a cup at a time, combining well with a wooden spoon. The result should be a slightly sticky dough that holds its shape.

Roll the dough into a ball using your hands and then place it between 2 large sheets of baking paper. Using a rolling pin, roll out the dough to around 3 mm (⅛ in) thick. Take a pig-shaped cookie cutter and cut shapes from the dough. Place onto the lined baking trays.

To make the glaze, combine the water and sugar in a small dish and brush the raw cookies with this syrup. Place the trays in the oven and bake for 10–12 minutes. Cool on wire racks before eating. You can dust the cookies with icing (confectioners') sugar while still hot, if desired.

These keep for a few days, stored in an airtight container.

Makes 30 piggies

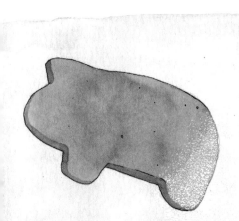
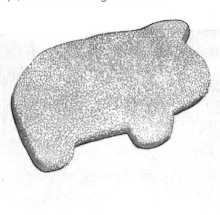
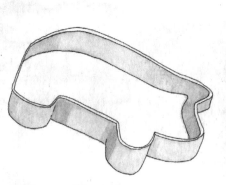

POLVORONES
• rich shortbread •

These are super-crumbly, sweet, melt-in-your-mouth round shortbreads usually eaten at Christmas, but they have become a staple in Mexican *panaderías* all year round.

150 g (5½ oz) margarine or butter
150 g (5½ oz) caster (superfine) sugar
300 g (10½ oz/2 cups) plain (all-purpose) flour
155 g (5½ oz/1½ cups) ground almonds

½ teaspoon aniseed, finely ground*
60 g (2 oz/½ cup) icing (confectioners') sugar or vanillin (a mixture of icing sugar and vanilla)

* Aniseed can be substituted with 1 teaspoon ground cinnamon, ½ teaspoon natural vanilla extract or ½ teaspoon lemon essence.

Preheat the oven to 250°C (480°F) and line a baking tray with baking paper.

Using an electric mixer, beat the margarine and caster sugar together until creamy and the sugar has dissolved. Add the flour, ground almonds and aniseed and mix until combined and the dough holds its shape.

On a lightly floured work surface or on baking paper, roll out the dough with a rolling pin to a 1 cm (½ in) thickness. Using a cookie cutter, cut round shapes (the traditional shape has scalloped edges like a flower).

Place the dough shapes on the baking tray and bake for 4–6 minutes or until starting to turn golden.

Remove from the oven and allow to rest for 1 minute, then transfer to a wire rack. Dust generously with the icing sugar while still hot and then allow to cool.

These will keep for up to 1 week in an airtight container.

Makes 20 cookies

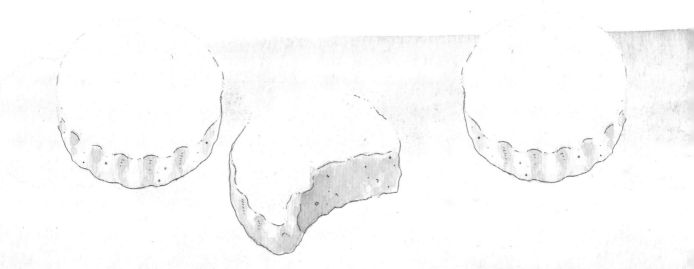

TORTA DE ELOTE

• corn cake •

A super-easy cake. Just put the ingredients in the blender, process and bake!

60 g (2 oz/½ cup) cornflour (cornstarch),
  plus extra for dusting
kernels from 4 corn cobs
450 ml (15 fl oz) condensed milk
4 eggs
100 g (3½ oz) butter, cut into small cubes
2 teaspoons baking powder

Preheat the oven to 180°C (350°F) and grease a 20 cm (8 in) square baking tin and dust lightly with cornflour.

Place the remaining ingredients in a blender or food processor and process until smooth.

Pour into the baking tin and bake in the oven for 50 minutes. Cool in the tin, or eat hot, straight from the oven.

Serve with ice cream.

This will keep for up to 1 week stored in the refrigerator.

Serves 8

TRENZAS CON MIEL

·honey braids·

When Abuelo would walk Mum and her sisters to their convent-based school, he would search his pockets for a few spare pesos to give the girls to spend at the school canteen. Mum would always buy these.

For the braids:

14 g (½ oz) dried yeast
60 ml (2 fl oz/¼ cup) warm water
200 ml (7 fl oz) milk
100 ml (3½ fl oz) vegetable oil
  (not olive oil)
55 g (2 oz/¼ cup) sugar
2 eggs, lightly beaten
700 g (1 lb 9 oz/4⅔ cups) strong flour
½ teaspoon salt

For the honey syrup:

125 ml (4 fl oz/½ cup) honey
110 g (4 oz/½ cup) sugar
125 ml (4 fl oz/½ cup) water

In a small bowl, mix the yeast and warm water. Set aside for 5 minutes. Once the yeast has started to bubble, transfer to a larger bowl and combine with the milk, vegetable oil, sugar and eggs. Mix well.

Sift in the flour and salt, then mix with your hands. Knead for around 10 minutes until smooth and elastic but not sticky. Place back in the bowl, cover with a clean tea towel (dish towel) and allow to rest in a warm spot for 1–2 hours, or until doubled in size.

Punch the dough to deflate and knead it again for 5–10 minutes or until very pliable and bubbles appear underneath the surface of the dough. Place the dough back in the bowl, cover with a tea towel and allow to double in size. When the dough is ready, divide it into 6 equal-sized portions. Roll each into a sausage shape. You should have 6 sausage-shaped pieces of dough, roughly the same size and thickness.

Preheat the oven to 200°C (400°F) and line a baking tray with baking paper.

Take 3 'sausages' and braid the pieces of dough together. Secure both ends by moistening the dough with a little milk and pinching the ends firmly. You should have 2 braids.

Place the braids on the lined baking tray, cover loosely with a tea towel and allow to rest for another hour. Bake in the oven for 15–20 minutes, or until the braids turn golden. Allow to cool slightly.

To make the honey syrup, place all the ingredients in a small saucepan and bring to the boil over a high heat stirring constantly. Reduce the heat to low and simmer for 7 minutes. Pour the syrup over the trenzas while the syrup is still hot, but allow to cool completely before serving. These keep for a couple of days stored in an airtight container.

Makes 2 braids

CANILLAS

·'skinny legs'·

These are devilishly buttery, delicate sweet
pastries that look like long sticks and are so easy to make.

2 teaspoons ground cinnamon
110 g (4 oz/½ cup) sugar
4 sheets of frozen puff pastry, thawed
60 g (2 oz) good-quality butter, melted

Preheat the oven to 180°C (350°F) and line a baking tray with baking paper.

Combine the cinnamon and sugar together in a bowl.

Brush 1 sheet of puff pastry with melted butter. Dust with the cinnamon and sugar
mix. Top with another sheet of pastry, and again brush with melted butter and sprinkle
the sugar mix on top. Repeat this process until all the pastry sheets have been used.

With a very sharp knife, cut the pastry in half, and then in half again, and so on until
you end up with 6 long strips of pastry measuring around 4 cm (1½ in) wide. Brush
the top of the pastries again with butter, sprinkle with the sugar mix and place on the
lined baking tray.

Bake for 12–15 minutes or until golden brown, puffed up and smelling delicious.
Remove from the tray and allow to cool on a wire rack.

These will keep for a few days in an airtight container.

Makes 6 canillas

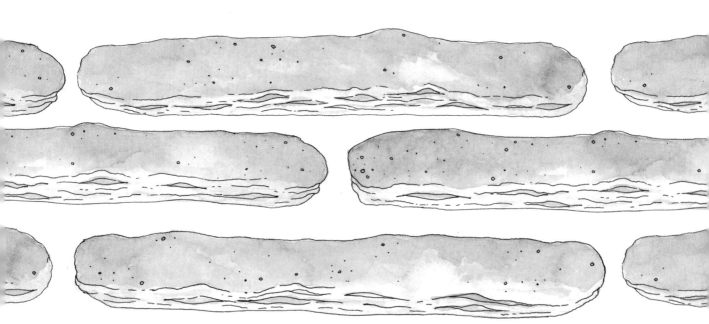

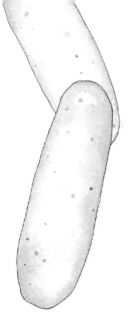

LENGUAS DE GATO

• 'cats' tongues' •

This is a very old recipe from my Spanish ancestors. The resulting lenguas de gato are delicate, sweet, light and crispy cookies, usually served with hot chocolate at *merienda* (snack) time.

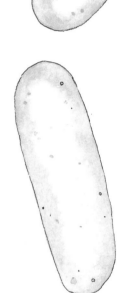

120 g (4½ oz) unsalted butter, melted
½ teaspoon natural vanilla extract
55 g (2 oz/¼ cup) caster (superfine)
  sugar
60 g (2 oz/½ cup) icing (confectioners')
  sugar
120 g (4½ oz) plain (all-purpose) flour
3 egg whites

Preheat the oven to 140°C (275°F) and line a baking tray with baking paper.

Combine the melted butter, vanilla and caster sugar and mix well until the sugar has dissolved. Add the icing sugar and mix until it has dissolved.

Mix in the flour, 1 tablespoon at a time. Add the egg whites and mix until well combined.

Set the mixture aside to rest for 1 hour.

Place the mixture into a piping (icing) bag and pipe 2 cm (¾ in) lengths onto the lined baking tray.

Bake in the oven for 6–8 minutes or until the edges of the lenguas are coloured. They will be very soft and fragile at this stage so allow them to cool before peeling them off the baking paper. The lenguas should be thin, crispy and glossy.

These will keep for a few days when stored in an airtight container.

Makes around 12

Variation: When piping the mixture, form 5 cm (2 in) rounds and bake as instructed. While the pastry is still hot, remove them from the paper, being careful not to break them, and drape them carefully over the back of a small glass or cup and allow to dry. The end result is an edible, delicious little 'basket' that can be filled with crème anglaise and fresh berries or other available fruit.

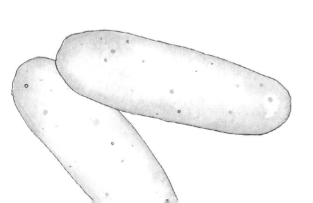

my sister Carmen with
our Australian & Mexican
grandfathers

at Los Arrayanes

my sister, Abuela & Abuelo

Abuelo's cousin, Abuela, Tino,
Abuela's sister Charito & Abuelo

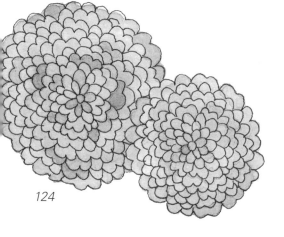

Carmen, Abuelo, me
& Abuelo's cousin at
La Granja

on the farm

in Alvarado

later years

¡Adios!

INDEX

CIUDAD DE MÉXICO

COMIDA DEL RANCHO

GOLOSINAS Y DULCES

PANADERÍA

An SBS book

Published in 2015 by Hardie Grant Books

Hardie Grant Books (Australia)
Ground Floor, Building 1
658 Church Street
Richmond, Victoria 3121
www.hardiegrant.com.au

Hardie Grant Books (UK)
5th & 6th Floor
52–54 Southwark Street
London SE1 1RU
www.hardiegrant.co.uk

A Cataloguing-in-Publication entry is available from the catalogue of the
National Library of Australia at www.nla.gov.au

My Abuelo's Mexican Feast
ISBN 978 1 74270 678 8

Designed and illustrated by Daniella Germain
Based on the recipes of Carmelita Ochoa de Hermida, Mexico

Publishing Director: Paul McNally
Project Editors: Meelee Soorkia and Rihana Ries
Editor: Ariana Klepac
Design Manager: Mark Campbell
Production Manager: Todd Rechner

Colour reproduction by Splitting Image Colour Studio
Printed and bound in China by 1010 Printing International Limited

Find this book on **Cooked.**
cooked.com.au
cooked.co.uk